ETHICS:

The
Possibility
of
Moral
Choice

ETHICS:

The Possibility of Moral Choice

By Paul M. Edwards

Reorganized Church of Jesus Christ of Latter Day Saints
Herald Publishing House
Independence, Missouri

Library of Congress Cataloging-in-Publication Data

Edwards, Paul M.
   Ethics: The Possibility of Moral Choice / by
   Paul M. Edwards.
     p.   cm.
   ISBN 0-8309-0490-5 : $15.00
   1. Ethics.   I. Title.
  BJ1025.E44 1987
  170—dc19

93 92 91   **2 3 4 5 6 7**

CONTENTS

PREFACE

The object of systems of morality is to take possession of human life, to save it from being abandoned to passion or allowed to drift at hazard, to give it happiness by establishing it in the practice of virtue...

—Matthew Arnold

Recently I taught a graduate class on ethics for a local university. I did so primarily for my own enjoyment at no salary, but officially I was representing the university. As a part of my usual introduction, I explained the importance of honesty and announced I would fail anyone who cheated on examinations. Unfortunately, during the final examination, I noted one young woman was "cheating" by reading partial answers from another student.

During the semester I had come to know her fairly well. She was in her late twenties and because of a recent divorce was the total support of herself and her two young children. She had recently been hired by a federal agency—one that makes life-and-death decisions. It was an excellent job with a long-term future provided she completed her master's degree by the starting date—some two weeks after the close of my class. She was scheduled to graduate on time needing only my ethics class to do so. When I confronted her, she begged to be "forgiven" and asked for another chance.

I consider myself reasonably humane. At the same time I am also very aware of the necessity for academic honesty. What is more, I do not want a government full of non-ethical persons making decisions about my life and death any more than I want treatment from surgeons who cheated on their sewing exam. There was no particular "need" for the ethics class for the job she was seeking. Certainly it is not a "required skill" on any job. The master's degree was a formality rather than a skill level. On the other hand, there was my own integrity and the university's dependence on me to maintain its standards. I had to make a decision and make it quickly. My decision would deeply affect her life and that of her children; as well, it would affect me, the university, and "universal" values.

What decision should I make? How should I decide? On what basis should a decision be made? What was involved in my decision?

This is a book about ethics. That means it is a book about choices and why we make them. Therefore, it is a book about freedom, for freedom is what decision and choice are all about. Unlike those (libertarians) who would remove any limitations placed on personal freedom, ethicists have a much more modest goal. Their aim is to help us make the very best use of whatever freedom we might have or might find thrust upon us. Everywhere we turn these days we discover we have "won" another freedom. What that means, of course, is that we have more and more choices to make. In our modern world personal freedoms, or at least personal opportunities, have become so vast we often find it hard to deal with them. In the midst of these choices many have discovered that responsible freedom is a matter of learning the nature of one's restrictions and of choosing those which we will allow to restrict us. We begin to understand Paul's difficulty: "I don't do the good I want to do . . . [but] the evil that I don't want to do" (Romans 7:15).

In those early whispers of time when an unkempt savage stopped running and managed to act in a way which suggested an immediate conclusion to her act, intelligence was activated. When the peace of such a savage was shattered by the belief that what she did in one moment of time would somehow make a difference at a later point in time, then intellectual faith was born. And while it must have required eons to occur, eventually such persons realized that this faith—this knowledge—gave them choices. And before too much longer, the realization dawned that choices gave them freedom. And eventually—maybe only partially—the freedom to choose carried with it responsibilities.

During this long history the civilized savage realized freedom is often controlled by the environment. Persons discovered they are sometimes determined by events they do not understand and which are often out of their control. The awareness of control balanced by a sense of responsibility became the basis for ethical inquiry and moral behavior. When persons have the freedom born of choice they pay for their freedom with ethical responsibilities. Those responsibilities arise from choices which are more appealing, better, or more correct than all the others. And thus persons are torn between what they desire and what to them is desirable.

From what little information humans have available, we conclude that neither the beasts of the fields nor the gods in their heavens are worried about values. For the beasts the lack of values is unimportant or at least simple. For the gods we identify, values are pronounced and are not a matter of question. Human beings, however, do worry about

9

values. They fuss and fret, build and destroy civilizations all in the name of values. It was this human trait which led the first-century philosopher, Epictetus, to claim "humans are animals with red cheeks." He meant, of course, that humans are embarrassed; they blush.

My father is a great blusher, suffering most of his life from his fear that some social recognition or minor social sin would embarrass him. He suffered first from the embarrassment and then from the further embarrassment caused by his blushing.

As he knew, blushing signifies an awareness of self. As well it is the response of how we measure up against others. This personal awareness of evaluation and judgment is a means by which we test ourselves. We check ourselves. And eventually we compare ourselves against other human beings. This comparison is often the source of embarrassment. It is also the source of values clarification.

Over the centuries our primary human response has been to allow the environment to mold us, to allow others to make many of these choices for us. In doing this we have tried to relieve the embarrassment that emerges from being different. Yet to be products of environment gives away the freedom. Thornton Wilder wrote of the "loneliness that accompanies independence and the uneasiness that accompanies freedom." He spoke of difficulty and isolation of standing for choices in the face of opposition—to be embarrassed. The opposite danger is to conform. And this is the danger we have been dealing with, though not all that well.

The greatest danger, of course, is not so much that the world will force us to conform to some established thought or behavior; that is bad enough. But that in our fears and in our desire for comfort, we will assume it is our wish to reject our larger responsibility. Giving away our freedom to others is a characteristic of the modern age.[1]

Martin Hollis blames modern science for having robbed the natural world of much of its appearance of moral purpose. Science, because it has begun to tell us so much about *why* things happen or *how* they come about, has tended to draw attention away from the idea of purpose which we so easily attached to the unknown. Thus we have replaced the mystery with the realization of causes and have all so quickly espoused a larger cause-and-effect model. At one time there was a tendency to assume that when a sparrow fell it was understood by means of the moral implications of the spiritual reference. Now the realization of a bird's heart attack or lung failure draws our attention to the cause for the bird's failure to fly rather than to consider the purpose of its falling.

Our moral response has been to translate the cause and effect into a sort of "customary ethics" reflecting choices of habit and tradition. It identifies as our cause, our ancestral habits which range in approach from the red-necked assumptions of Archie Bunker to the more poetic and moderate comments of the Apostle Paul: "For as many as have sinned without law shall also perish without law; and as many as have sinned in the law shall be judged by the law" (Romans 2:12).

We call these responses "common sense" even though they are neither common nor do they often make any sense. When we use the word *common* we usually mean something held in common (that is, a lot of people believe it) or something that is low or simple so that everyone understands it. Such tradition rises from heritage, out of myths as well as experience, and reflects our grandfathers and mothers, aunts and all. This is a wisdom of experience passed on by generations and known in modern terminology as "parental recordings." By the word *sense* we mean feeling, or understanding, even though most often it is *acquired* information.

Reflective ethics, however, is the result of conscious reasoning rather than tradition or intuition. Such ethics are based on principles that have been established by consideration, reasoning, logic, and/or cognitive procedures. They are not so much rules, unless the rules themselves are the conclusion of such inquiries. Rather, reflective ethics are the result of looking carefully at particular problems and trying to reason out an answer to those problems. They reflect the need to understand in order to establish priorities. Gasset writes

This is simply that the generations are born one of another in such a way that the new generation is immediately faced with the forms which the previous generation gave to existence. Life, then, for each generation, is a task of two dimensions, one of which consists in the reception, through the agency of previous generations, or what has had life already, e.g., ideas, values, institution and so on, while the other is the liberation of the creative genius inherent in the generation concerned.[2]

Socratic Assumptions

Behind the idea of a "common universal" is the belief that whatever common knowledge of ethics is "generally" held is a product of what is called the "Socratic Assumptions." This view, expressed in *Crito* (Plato), emerges from the account of the philosopher's impending death for crimes against the state. In his closing statement Socrates reviews the moral code that has been with him during his life. The assumptions are basically these:

1. Our decisions about behavior must be based on honest facts; therefore, we must avoid decision-making on the basis of emotions. As much as is humanly possible, we must think clearly and rationally, basing our consideration on what factual information we have.

2. We must avoid the temptation to make our decisions on the basis of an adaptation of the common-sense view. The common mind is usually wrong. It is not because the common mind is bad or ignorant—far from it. But persons are generally uninformed, particularly about the decision they are trying to make. Often because the common understanding is generalized, persons seek decisions based on memories, not intelligence or courage about the future.

3. We should never do that which is morally wrong. This seems obvious but it is to be seen as a warning not a statement of fact. Our attention is drawn to the fact we must be concerned not only with decision-making but with avoiding the violation of a particular wrong.[3]

Speaking to Our Times

While ethical decisions have been around since men and women first began taking values seriously, there have been few times in human history when there has been so much demand for serious and intelligent thought about our ethical situation. The complexity of the modern world is such that it raises questions that would have been unheard of fifty years ago. The ability to do more things raises serious questions about whether we should do those things. A decision which President Franklin Delano

Roosevelt had to make earlier in World War II about the making of the atom bomb which was later used on Japan is an example. Advancing knowledge calls upon the modern person to seek to know what is right in the midst of such vastly complicated subjects as gene transplants, organ banks, and the use of atomic power. It is a time when significant decisions are being made which affect the whole world. Thus it is a time when we need a revitalization of rational thought about behavior. Certainly if the RLDS Church is to make a difference in the world it seeks to serve, it must take ethics seriously.

Recently while serving as a guest lecturer at a class on medical ethics, I heard a story—apocryphal, I hope—that illustrates the complex and awesome nature of the ethical questions facing our society. A young husband and wife discovered that the man was having trouble with his kidney. He would need a kidney transplant if he were to have much life after middle age. The couple had planned to have no children because they wanted to spend their money and their time on their own activities. However, after receiving this news, the man realized that he had no family—no brothers or sisters from whom a transplant would be successful. Thus, the couple decided to have a child for the sole purpose of providing a kidney for the father at the time it was needed. Certainly an ethical question. And certainly one for the 1990s.

Is Ethics Hard?

Ethical behavior is hard. And the study of ethics can be very difficult. It is true that one does not need to be an artist to enjoy the rainbow. For the enjoyment of primary colors one does not need to know all there is about them or to be aware of each and every distinction between appearance and reality. However, if any want to go beyond that to where they can appreciate art or the process of artistic creation, then it is important to learn a great deal about personal expression. At that point the subtleties and distinctions become important in a way that goes beyond appreciation.

So it is with most things humans do. The more we study the more we need to appreciate that there are often basic concepts and understandings available for our enlightenment. With further study we can appreciate much which will be of aid to us even if we do not completely understand all that the study means.

It was Hegel, I believe, who was often accused of providing too much information. "If you asked him how to get to town he would draw you a map of Europe" they would say. This is somewhat the problem I have here. I run the risk of telling most people far more than they want to know about choices and problems in relationships. In this case, as in so many, the author must fully understand in order to make the reader think it is simple. But underlying the fact that ethics can be understood is the belief that the readers *want* to understand, that they will make some effort to understand, and finally that they—that is the author and the reader—share an interest in ethical behavior.

I have proceeded on the assumption that you want to know more than you do about ethics, but that you do not wish to be blown over with the heavy winds of too many details and too much complex definition. Somewhere is a balance to be sought between detail and understanding.

Ethics is a branch of the larger philosophical discipline. As such, it has its own terminology as well as its own internal arguments about the exact meaning of words. Between introducing you to all this "garbage" and not discussing enough to help, I have hovered trying to deal with both my questions and yours. To the better informed this may seem simplistic and I apologize in advance; to the overly burdened who think I have said far too much, I seek their patience.

Author's Comments

It seems only ethical that the reader have some idea of the author's bias. My philosophical orientation is personalistic, at times slightly existential. These assumptions will affect this study no matter how carefully I try to be objective. I believe that an individual's own existence is always of immediate concern and that human questions are based on this interest and concern. In philosophy this is called the "egocentric predicament." This is not a condemnation of persons nor even a suggestion of selfish intent, but rather is an acknowledgment of the self-centeredness of all humans. This work is written from the perspective of this predicament. Persons at least begin with concern for their own interests.

I also believe morality is primarily learned. Most of us would agree that people are social animals; that is, they are creatures who seek society. And we are inclined to find our codes of behavior within that social framework. It is my conviction that morality is not innate in human beings, that is, it is not born within us. Rather morality is discovered and invented as a part of our response to creation and our adjustment to life. While I agree that persons are not born sinful either (the fact of being born is not to be seen as sin), I do confess it seems to me they are born with desires and expectations that must be harnessed. Such persons are born with the propensity for learning, order, and evaluation through which they discover right, wrong, good, and bad. Such evaluations are learned in the struggle as life writes a series of messages upon the fairly clean slate of human consciousness.

What persons do have is an inherent sense of the universal. They are aware of the universal nature of both their humanness and their creation. And in that awareness of the universal they find the seemingly inherent commonality of their discoveries. Thus, while they may well have to discover—or perhaps it is uncover—their moral understandings, such understandings take upon them a universal nature in both the discovery and execution. I am not ignorant of the fact that there is a major problem in discussing the creation of universals or in suggesting that one might compile such universals. There is a general consensus among philosophers that persons uncover (discover) such universals. That is, the universals are there and we, in our search, may well discover them. The absolute nature of what we define as universal comes into serious question when I suggest that they are more "recognized" than uncovered. Likewise when I suggest they are more identified than discovered. Perhaps at some later time an explanation of this paradoxical dilemma might be made. At the moment it is only necessary to identify it for the reader.

I also maintain that a certain amount of doubt is necessary for an emerging moral theory. If one has only positive beliefs about such things, then there is

17

no opportunity for reflection. Ethical theory emerges when men and women are confronted with the necessity of making decisions about things for which they have no firm undergirdings. Persons change, they alter environments, they experience shattering grief and breathtaking joy. All of these affect the nature of their ground of understanding.

At these points the customary tools may not suffice and it is here that persons are called upon to identify the central issues. Once identified they can be tested against assumptions and values, and one can determine a course of action.

It is of significance, however, to note that without the ability to ask serious questions and to deal with the struggle of ethical decisions, persons quickly become slaves to, and thus enslaved by, the conflict of ethical values inherent in customary ethics. Examples include: the woman who is required to choose between silence over white-collar crime and her loyalty to friends; the man who must choose between the needs of his wife and those of his children; a person who must face the conflict between serving on a jury as a civic duty and personal feelings regarding capital punishment. These are serious issues that require an ability to see each case and make ethical decisions.

Quiz

At the end of each chapter I have provided a short quiz, either matching tests, True-and-False, or fill-in-the-blank (short essay) type. The quiz is provided for those readers who like to check themselves to see if they understand the material or if they are digesting what the author has provided. Try them for your own sake; you might be surprised how much you have added to your information. After you have finished, look up the answers in the book.

Acknowledgments

Anytime a book is written it is a joint effort. Many of the persons who help don't know that, for they have contributed in a way that can never be acknowledged. Their contribution lies in the effect they have had on me over the years: in shaping my thinking, in uttering a word or a phrase so often that I began to think it was mine. I have acknowledged this where I could, but offer my thanks to them all and hope that in some small way I can return the favor.

In addition are those who have offered more obvious aid. To persons who have helped by their presence and to those who simply did not get in the way, I am thankful. I must express my appreciation to the early breakfast staff at Shoney's restaurant in Independence for that is where the majority of this work was written. My thanks as well to Beverly Spring and her *aide-de-combatants:* Nancy, Becky, Sharon, Jill, Penny, Sue, and Debbie. And to the executives of Temple School who, aware of my time frame, chuckled quietly. And to Carolynn for the usual—thus most significant—reasons.

* * *

If such a volume can be dedicated, this one is affectionately offered in memory of my dear friend, Dr. Newell Yates of Graceland College, Lamoni, Iowa, a moral man in an amoral world.

End Notes

1. Harold Dodds, "The Importance of Being an Individual," *Wisdom* (July 1956), 53.
2. Jose Ortega Gasset, *Man and Crisis* (New York: Norton Library 1962), 16.
3. John Dewey, "Reflective Morality and Ethical Theory" in William Frankena and John T. Granrose, *Introductory Readings in Ethics* (Englewood Cliffs, New Jersey: Prentice Hall 1974), 18–21.

CHAPTER 1
WHAT IS ETHICS?

*Morality is man's endeavor to harmonize
conflicting interests.*

—Ralph Perry

Many literate people can trace their love of literature to a positive response to some particular work
or author. I admit to such a mentor, even a passion.
To me Victor Hugo's wonderful story *Les Miserables*
is such a work. I first read it (saw it) in *Classic
Comics* when I was seven or eight years of age
and was so intrigued with it that I followed my
mother to the old Kansas City Library in search of
the real thing. I discovered there a magic place
which allowed me to own this book for two weeks. I
returned home with what was to be the first of
many copies of the novel. *Les Miserables*[1] is an
elegant story of human beings and of good and evil.
It is vastly melodramatic and overly romantic as be-
fitting its times and is a morality play on the purpose of being human in the face of consistent human failure.

Like much literature of that period, the story is
complicated and the list of characters runs on like a
small-town phone directory. Jean Valjean, the hero,
was arrested as a young man for stealing a loaf of
bread to feed his widowed sister and her large family. Through the harshness of the nineteenth-
century French penal systems, he spent nearly
nineteen years in payment. On his release he steals
the silverware of a saintly bishop who has be-

21

friended him. When caught and returned to the bishop for charging, the bishop tells the police he has given the thief the silver thus keeping Valjean from jail. The lie is repaid by Jean Valjean's decision to follow the laws of God, or at least those of charity and kindness. He steals only one more time. This time he lifts a sack of silverware taken from a large rich church to aid the good bishop in his work.

Valjean's final conversion comes through his affection for a young orphan whom he eventually makes his ward and whom, on several occasions, he protects with his own life. During a long and complex life Valjean is faced with choices concerning his own silence—thus his own safety—and acts of goodness and human charity. On one occasion he risks return to jail rather than allowing another to go in his name. He protects a young man from his own folly and the rigors of the French Revolution because of the man's love of Cosette, Valjean's ward. And eventually, when all his efforts at goodness seem to have worked against him, he lies brokenhearted and dying. In a deathbed scene that would bring tears to Rambo, he is reconciled with his ward and passes on to his own rewards. He was no saint but a human figure worn down, as well as lifted up, by his decisions.

In this story, as in much of life, the ethical judge is the observer. A serious reader is constantly faced with the questions: What do you think you would have done? How do you feel? Is stealing food to feed your family bad? And what is the difference between stealing food and stealing candlesticks? Do the massive injustices suffered by this man justify any rewards or punishments?

To most persons the statement ''dishonest is bad''

seems to be obvious. There is seldom any debate about it. Part of the reason is the language; dishonesty is defined in the dictionary as the "lack of adherence to a moral code." The serious ethical question is not *if* honesty is good or bad but *what* is honest or dishonest. Much of the decision lies in whether we call something dishonest or not. This is true in many respects. Murder, for example, means to "take a life unjustifiably"; assuming, then, if the person talking can justify the death then it is not considered murder. The taking of a life in punishment of other crimes is considered by many persons to be justifiable and thus the killing is not murder.

Probably Valjean did not report to his sister that he was evil or had done something wrong. What he was doing was not evil for him. On the other hand, even when stealing we may still believe that it is wrong and should not be done. Usually, however, we suggest to ourselves that in this particular case *this* is not stealing. Perhaps, you could say that taking something that does not belong to you, but which provides a good consequence (like taking a knife away from a small child) is not stealing. However, taking something from someone which produces a bad consequence (like taking their food) is stealing.

We usually assume that while stealing is bad it is also bad to break one's promise—as to one's spouse and child about providing them supper or to allow someone to die (the logical outcome of not eating)—so that the question of stealing becomes more a question of degree. It is also a matter of degree when we say that it is not *really* stealing to pocket two pennies found on the table, but to *pick up* 10 million laying there is a capital crime. Is it the

23

act of stealing or the consequences that determine if an act is ethical?

This chapter is about ethics and the study of moral behavior. As we have seen, many persons use the term *ethics* to suggest behavior that stems from a determination of right or wrong. It is used primarily to mean a set of rules or standards. This certainly is a good beginning to our study but our understanding needs to be taken further to show that ethics is more a study of principles about good and bad actions.

Ethics

Generally considered, ethics is a standard by which individuals or a community regulate the behavior of its members. These rules or standards are used to determine what is respectful, acceptable, and in the final analysis, legitimate. And, of course, what is not. Such a definition goes from the set of "rules or good ideas" for a social club to a systematic universal system which might be expressed by a church. Several definitions are available.

- To a philosopher it might mean

  The investigation into fundamental principles which are, or ought to be, found in a given field of human endeavor and which provide standards for human behavior.

- To a classical ethicist it means

  The set of principles recognized by an existing group, and the recognition that these principles are practical rather than theoretical.

- In the philosophical dictionary ethics is

  A set of standards by which a particular group or community decides to regulate its behavior—to distinguish what is legitimate or acceptable in pursuit of their aim from what is not.[2]

- In Darrell Reeck's *Ethics for Professionals,* it is
  The art of reflection on the moral meaning of human action.
- For Paul Lehmann in *Ethics in a Christian Context*
  Christian ethics, as a theological discipline, is the reflection upon the question, and its answer: What am I, as a believer in Jesus Christ and as a member of his Church, to do?[3]

Ethics and Morality

There is a great deal of confusion between the terms ethics and morality. Perhaps some clarification would be helpful. The simplest way to end the confusion would be to assume they are two words for the same thing. But rain and snow are just two words for the same thing—water. Yet the degree of difference is meaningful, especially when you are heading for rush-hour traffic. For the ethicists the difference between ethics and morality is significant. *Ethics is the study of the general principles behind specific moral choices.* It is the study of the character of morality and deals with the essence of such morals. Such a study may well result in the identification of principles. *Morals are concerned with the goodness or badness of particular human action (acts).* Ethics is interested in the standards by which the act is judged.

Ethics, then, is bound to be primarily theoretical. It deals with abstract questions that go beyond tradition and community rules to raise inquiries about the assumptions on which those actions are based. It is at this point that the study of ethics begins to question if we are led by generic understanding or if we inherit rules or establish them by vote. Ethics deals with the larger principles upon which we act.

Both words have origins that reflect their current meaning. Ethics comes from the Greek word *ethike* which has been translated as meaning the science of character. Morality is derived from the Latin *mos* or *mores* which we have taken to mean manners, or perhaps custom. Thus we have come to use the words in their technical sense to mean that ethics is the study of what it means to be moral, and morality is the act of putting that inquiry into practice.

The Study of Ethics

The study of ethics, like the study of any human endeavor, is complicated. Basically, however, it involves two parts. One is the study of specific moral and ethical problems. The second is the study of morality in general. In the early phases of philosophy these two were rarely separated but in the last century philosophy has realized that they are different questions. The first, the study of particular ethical problems, is usually called *normative ethics*. This refers to the specific questions of what one does about particular cases of sexual behavior, wars, justice, or whatever. The second is called *metaethics*—meaning beyond ethics—and deals with the nature and justification of ethics. In this book the two are tied together by using specific examples while trying to deal with larger questions.

Alison was a hard-working and responsible young woman. She had completed her college and had a job at the beginning level as an artist for a greeting card company in a large city. She hoped that someday she would be able to branch out on her own and do freelance work. Eventually—if everything worked out—she wanted to spend the majority of her time painting seriously. In the meantime she needed to make a living, pay her own way, and save for her goal. She was very conscious of her money, limited as it was, for in effect it was her ticket to freedom.

Her mother lived some 300 miles away. It was hard for Alison to leave home but it had been harder on her mother. As a concession Alison had formed the habit of calling home every Sunday night to let her mother know everything was all right. Communication was an expensive activity, and her mother had suggested Alison call home, let it ring, and if it was answered ask for her father who had been dead nearly ten years. Her mother then would recognize that the girl was all right and simply say that the man was no longer living. Thus they would communicate but the phone company would not charge them anything.

Alison really felt the need to assure her mother. Particularly since at their last conversation Alison was still smarting because one of her supervisors had adopted her idea and submitted it as his own. When it came time to call, Alison decided to call from a pay phone in order to make it easier and she dialed the number. When her mother answered she asked for the father by name. The expected reply came and the girl hung up. She had made her mother happy, relieved whatever anxieties might have built up, and had not spent any money.

This scenario, however strained, brings up several questions of morality and ethics. Using it as an effort to understand ethics and morality, let us take a closer look. The question about her actions: "Shall I

27

use the phone but not pay for it?" is a question of morality for it asks if it is correct to make a free call. The question of determining if her need is greater than the phone company's need to be paid may well involve an ethical question. Questions about value or her rights in not being able to call, or the phone company's rights in having the services used without paying are ethical questions. The particular act of moral violation expresses a general principle of right and wrong.

Ethics should not be confused with moral theology, despite the assumptions we are inclined to make. Both cover the same ground and are involved in our lives. Moral theology elevates the inquiry to a higher plane making it more serious, more significant, more "people touching." It considers right and wrong from the transcendental point of view. Moral theology has revelation on its side and thus is able to make pronouncements about behavior even though there is as much discussion about the facts of moral theology as there are about any major ideas. But our concern here is about ethics and we shall stay with that discussion as much as possible.

Why the Question?

Ethics is concerned with *why*. Why is something right or wrong? What constitutes right or good? Why or how does this particular act apply to larger rules or decisions we might have made? It is concerned with the process by which we make moral claims or rules, and the means by which we determine them if we can, and how we will apply them. Ethics then is the tool, or the procedure, for doing morality and moral theology and is necessary for the moral reasoning of a society.

There is another kind of question. This question concerns values. It results from our concern about what a term like "good" means. If bad is more or less significant than good, are we considering questions of more than one right at a time, or conflicting rights between persons? Ethics is concerned with questions about mind, and questions of "can" (able), and "what if." Such questions are addressed to what sort of community we want, or what type of person we wish to be. How can I use my talents and abilities in the manner which will best serve humanity? And of course, what right do I have to decide what is best for other persons?

Ethics Versus Law

Another point to keep in mind is that law (civil and criminal) is not ethics. To be legal is not necessarily to be ethical.

When coming to my office from Kansas City I need to turn right off Lexington onto River Boulevard. At that stop light there is a sign which announces in no uncertain terms, NO TURNS ON RED. It fails to take into account that there is little or no traffic. As I sit there waiting for the light to change so I can turn, wondering if everyone in the city has left, I keep thinking that I *should* go ahead and turn. There is no traffic; there is no observable policeman; there is no "intent" of the law being broken. After all, the law exists because during the brief World Conference period every two years it is dangerous to have persons turning into traffic at this point. But now, there is no danger.

If I go ahead and turn I have broken the law. But have I done wrong? There is a difference between the law and ethics. If I break the law and that

29

policeman I didn't think was there catches me, then he will fine me and perhaps even take away my license. I have been punished. But, more realistically, I have paid for the privilege of breaking the law. The law says in effect, "the society does not want you turning there. But if you want to turn badly enough, you are going to have to pay." The hope is that if you pay significantly and often enough you will soon decide it is better to do what society wants you to do.

Ethically, however, the wrong that I might have done is not excused by my willingness to pay the price. If I am a good citizen then I might well assume that to break the law is unethical, and to turn on a red light is wrong as well as being illegal. However, if I assume that as a good steward of my time I cannot afford to sit at the light counting seconds when I should be at the office writing ethics courses, then I may well decide that while it is illegal to turn right it is not necessarily unethical. I may well remain a good person even if I am a criminal. Civil disobedience falls into this category.[4]

Terminology

When we read something new we will run into words (terminology) that are unfamiliar. Often what we think of as "big words" are nothing more than new words. We should not let them scare us away. Note the following illustrations I came across this past week:

"Boot PC-DOS, enter the data and wait for the 'A prompt'"

—IBM PC Manual (instructions)

"If we are to avoid this foundationalist conclusion we shall have to show the regress argument is fallacious."

—Dancy on *Epistemology* (textbook)

"...pureed vegetables to braised beef mixture before broiling. Serve with coddled or poached eggs, scones or croquettes, and fruit frapee."

—Eileen Terril (cooking)

"Analysis, measure of central tendency, dispersion, and correlation, estimation and hypothesis testing, bivariate regression, elementary ANOVA."

—Graceland College (catalog)

"An excellent canape of mushrooms, mousse de truite, bibb lettuce with Kiwi meringue and vacherin de fruit, or pate chaud."

—Kansas City Restaurant Guide (menu)

"To park an established call confirm after location PARK 57 1219 in alphanumeric display, if idle, otherwise."

—Siemens Telephone Directory (directions)

If you know much about computers you will recognize in the first example that we are being told to turn on the computer so that it looks in the main drive for whatever disk is there and loads the "bootstrap program" stored on the disk. This will place its instructions and procedures into the memory and buffers of the computer. And those familiar with the others understand them as well. When trying to use a cookbook I ask an expert—my

31

wife—to translate it into English. The point is, most human endeavors have their own terms.

In the study of ethics there are words which seem hard and which may discourage you. However, if you give them a little thought and use them, just like the words in the restaurant guide or cooking directions, they will become familiar and appear much easier.

Facts of Moral Life

Ethics does not take place in a vacuum nor on cloud nine. There are some facts of moral life that need to be understood.

1. Everyone makes ethical or moral decisions. The tendency is to assume that if they are not large decisions then, in some respect, they are not difficult, nor do they reflect life behavior. This is not true. Everyone makes decisions every day in hundreds of different ways, all of which affect and effect their lives.

2. There are some things for which we are not responsible—that is, we did not cause them—but for which we are accountable. The most basic of these, of course, is life itself. As far as we know we did not create our own lives. But most would agree that we are accountable for how our lives are spent, what is done with them, and in a legal and moral sense how we use them.

3. Morality changes, grows, fails, is replaced, and repeats itself just like everything else. Moral fashions change. The most obvious illustration is in the area of sexual morals. The only consistent thing about changing cultural concepts of sexual practice is the almost universal ban on incest. But there is little else that has not, at some point, altered.

4. And last, but not least, living in connection with other persons means that there must be some agreements. Just how many agreements and to what degree they are accepted is open to question. But if more than one person must live in the same area they must come to some agreement on how they are going to get along.

Failure of Ethics

Philosophy is a fairly unique discipline in that it is often its own subject matter. The role of the philosopher is not only to question such things as what is ethical, but also to seriously question if the study of ethics (or metaphysics, or whatever) itself is a worthwhile activity for the human mind. This self-analysis was going on even before Socrates himself asked the questions. But within the last twenty years there has been a great deal of concern about the study of ethics in particular. The concerns are serious and should at least be mentioned here. For the sake of simplicity I shall mention only four.

1. There appears to be an increasing loss of faith in human beings—both, I am sure, from a fundamental religious point of view and an existential point of view. The first says persons are incapable of their own salvation and allows that God will need to save persons by total grace. The second agrees that human effort will not save us but is convinced God will not save us either. What it says is that human beings have lost faith in their own ability to deal with situations. This loss of faith challenges the ability of science to provide technological answers to the many problems we face as a society. It is a challenge to the ability of reason to work out the difficulties we face in decision-making. This loss is a

challenge to the emotional stability of persons to deal with the conflicts of human relationships. But most of all it reflects an increased willingness of persons to give in to the situation, whatever it may be, with no effort to control or change what is happening.

2. Second, an increasing willingness to suspend the intellect for the sake of action. The frustration which results in the fixability of human situations leads us to the need to act—to do something even if it is wrong. Often the thing that we do is to ignore the intellect—and with it the use of reason to control emotion—and revert to animal instincts. One of the paradoxes of society is that persons must now live down the kinds of behavior that made civilization possible. One major reason humans control the universe as we know it is because we have been meaner and tougher as well as smarter, and more and more willing to walk over the weak to get what we want. Now civilization suggests being "human" is not to be meaner, tougher, smarter. We should stress commonality and allow the weak to survive—in fact help them—to be victorious over the strong.

Now, as human concern over the nature of the world catches up to us, our inclination is to revert to the animal characteristics that brought us control in the first place. The clash is on. Reason, which has so often been our moderator—however poorly it did the job—has been weakened. In its place passion takes over.

3. A third failure hits close to home for religious persons, and the church should be more interested in this than in most other things. It is simple. We have made no preparation for modernity. We have

34

stressed the need for work-related skills, have built universities and institutes in the name of success, have developed every productive talent we can think of in the name of progress, yet have watched uncaringly while schools ceased to teach values, while universities failed to teach decision-making and choice selection, while freedom was given away to the efficiency of commonality. The reason we have such poor ethical abilities is that we do not prepare ourselves to be people for ethical tasks. It is often pointed out that to be a plumber in any of the United States you need a license but in most states you need no training whatsoever to make ethical and moral decisions. That is why our plumbing works far better than our ethics.

4. Finally, philosophers warn that we have given into what has been identified as "shoddy pragmatism or sophomoric dogmaticism." This harsh criticism identifies the tendency to accept as good anything which works. An act is identified as right if it produces results. To lie for the sake of success—as stereotyped by the used car salesman but more probably true of admissions officers at colleges—is criticized only on the basis of whether the lie will work, not on the basis of the rightness or wrongness of the lie.

When you think of the number of people in the United States today who are employed for the express purpose of misleading or telling half-truths or outright lies it makes one wonder about the source of value.[5]

Quiz
1. What is the difference between a legal act and an ethical one?

2. Describe what makes an ethical question metaethics?
3. Is moral behavior necessarily legal?
4. What is civil disobedience?
5. Define normative ethics.
6. Define theology.
7. Refresh your memory on the "Facts of Moral Life." Can you add any others to the list?

End Notes

1. Victor Hugo, *Les Miserables*, (1862).
2. Anthony Flew (Ed.), *A Dictionary of Philosophy* (New York: St. Martin's Press 1979), 104.
3. Paul Lehmann, *Ethics in a Christian Context* (New York: Harper and Row, 1963), 17.
4. The whole contrast between law is very complicated. If you are interested I would recommend that you check in Plato's *Republic* for a discussion of this confrontation.
5. Bruce Wilshire, "Fifty Years of Academic Philosophy in the United States: Why the Failure of Nerve?" *Soundings* Vol. 67, No. 4, 1984, 411–419.

CHAPTER 2

FREEDOM AND MATTERS OF CHOICE

The central question which each of us now faces will remain; will perhaps be more acute: what shall I do with the freedom I have?
—Russell Shaw

Lyman Cobb was trying to make an important decision. The importance was not so much the acts he was forced to choose between—whether to use an illegal list of answers to a forthcoming law test—but with the vocational choice he had made. He saw this particular decision reflecting the larger question. Remembering his mother's advice, he decided to make a list of the reasons for and against. At the top of the page he wrote *Ultimate Purpose.* Then on the left side of the page he wrote "For" (meaning to accept the illegal information) and on the right side "Against." After a moment's thought he realized he was not sure of his purpose, and proceeded to make his list. On the left he included such things as "It is immoral" and "I might get caught." On the right side were such things as "the test is stupid anyway" and "if I don't pass I will not get my degree."

Most of us have done this in one form or another. And chances are, like Lyman Cobb, we will soon discover the list of "for" and "against" makes little sense if we do not know what the ultimate purpose is: that is, the purpose one has in mind, the reason for making a choice, the limitations and opportunities in the outcome of the action. To decide whether an act, or the consequence of an act, is good or bad is often very closely related to what you are trying to accomplish, where you are going, what sort of person you want to be, and what the purpose is of the decision.

If Cobb's purpose is to be a good lawyer, then the test is a means for him to judge his growth and understanding and make some decisions about study habits and procedures. If his purpose is to make a lot of money at a prestigious law firm, then the test is an obstacle that needs to be overcome. If his purpose is to do well in school as its own reward, then to cheat on the examination would defeat his whole reason to be there. On the other hand, if Cobb's point is to impress the ladies of his class with his high grades, then knowing the answers in advance may well serve his purpose.

Freedom

I believe the vast majority of persons have freedom as their ultimate good. However, it is difficult to know just what people mean by the freedom they desire. Obviously there are many degrees of freedom as well as numerous kinds. We take it for granted that others are free to make most of their choices and so we hold them responsible for their actions. Likewise we feel guilty about our own mistakes; thus, in our minds at least, we feel we could have acted in a different manner.

It is also true that we feel very much controlled, and determined by things. We are forced into actions by events beyond our control—the economics of our birth for example—and are often molded by the environment. We say that "we are trapped" meaning that no choice seems available which will satisfy all the demands placed by the pressures upon us. This problem of conflicting convictions about freedom and determinism is reflected in Christian theology. In traditional Christianity these two positions are held with equal fervor: persons are free and thus responsible for their sins, and God is all powerful and the determiner of every event including our lives.

Sir Arthur Eddington, one of the leading scientific spokesmen of my early generation, remarked "this is one of man's oldest riddles. How can the independence of human volition be harmonized with the fact that we are integral parts of a universe which is subject to the rigid order of Nature's laws?" Of course, neither the freedom nor the determinism is complete or pure. In many respects we live in both worlds—damning one or the other. We are conscious of numerous limitations upon us even while we pursue the freedom that makes ethics possible.

Perhaps the primary limitations are those which come from within us. They are the products of our own natures and they alter and even prevent our choice. They could be habits or illness or psychological or even philosophical hang-ups. Limitations that originate from outside of us, from externals or environments, are identified as secondary. They are not secondary because they are less important but because they are outside our control. Perhaps we should look at a few of these limitations more clearly.

To a significant degree our freedom tends to be restricted by the nature of things. Obviously our physical freedom is limited by the nature of our physical make-up. The reality of our creation makes

39

it hard—if not impossible—to fly, run very fast, walk upside down for long, to squeeze ourselves through the eye of a needle. Handicapped persons could explain to us numerous ways in which their freedom is restrained by the limitations of the handicaps. The very fact of being (that is, having a body) puts us in a position where we can envision or desire activities that are physically impossible.

In somewhat the same manner we are restricted by our environment. As I write, the wet snow of a midwestern winter is accumulating on the streets. By midnight the roads will be nearly impassable and much of the freedom of movement enjoyed by persons in this city will be lost. As a midwesterner I am not free to walk on the beach or climb mountains in my backyard. On the other hand, I am not limited by massive traffic jams or weeks of dense fog.

Another set of limitations is present because of our "expectant" environment. I require mental and physical comfort and relief from oppressive factors. I also find myself less free because of my psychological attachment to them. Because I want shelter from the rain and the snow, I soon discover new limitations imposed on me by the problems of a home. Because I am afraid, I am inclined to purchase security at the cost of independence.

The same sort of balance exists as we trade freedom in the political dimension. In the United States persons enjoy a great deal of personal freedom which is defined as the right to have unrestricted actions. By this we mean speech, assembly, motion, disagreement, and even the freedom of disrespect. These are purchased, as we all know, by surrendering other freedoms. We trade the freedom of unrestricted activity (submission to laws) for freedom from worry about, or suffering from, other's unrestrained activities. We trade our freedom to drive without a license for the freedom to drive free from unlicensed drivers on our roads. As we say, "My freedom to swing my fist ends where someone else's nose begins."

For large segments of the world, the question of political freedom is much more severe. In some totalitarian societies one's freedom is traded for life. To preserve life, secure some modicum of safety, or retain even a limited standard of living one is forced to accept unlimited restrictions on movement, behavior, and thought. But regardless of our political situation our personal freedom is limited or expanded by the power of goverment. At any level we have granted a portion of our freedom in return for help in keeping other portions. We have bargained for freedom.

We have mentioned only three suggestions concerning limitations on our freedom. There are many more and they are imposed by many things: ourselves, history, creed and dogmas, reality, time, others, economics, metaphysical and cosmic causes, or needs.

Standing in opposition to these limitations is our concern for self-determination—our desire to "do our own thing." Granted, no one is totally unaware of the reality of limitations. And even though persons are inclined to suggest a desire for total personal freedom, there is no way in the world they could survive it if they obtained it—or would they want to. If the local police force had such freedom, or the drivers on the interstate highway, or the clerks in the bank, or the nurses in the emergency room, life would be in such a shambles that the disorder itself would create massive limitations on our freedom.[1]

Limits of Self-Being

Given that this is true, we still have considerable individual ability to exercise freedom. Ethics depends on the assumption that at some critical point persons have the freedom to choose. In the church the term agency is most often used for this conviction (Genesis 7:40 and Doctrine and Covenants 58:60).

One of the most powerful restrictions upon us is the pressure of self-determinism. In my reading somewhere, I ran across the story of a wise, old teacher who was sitting quietly on a mountainside talking with his student. After a while they both noticed a scorpion had gotten itself caught under the edge of a rock which was just big enough to have trapped the small, violently poisonous insect. The old teacher removed the rock. The scorpion, scared and lashing out, stung the old man. It was certain death.

"Why did you do that?" the student demanded. "Didn't you know what the insect would do?"

"My son," he said, "just because I knew how the scorpion would act is no reason for me not to act as I would. I can no more refuse to save its life than it could refuse to take mine."

Self-determinism* is the manner by which persons mold themselves through their own choices. It is also the manner in which a person is determined by the making of decisions. Only one choice is the

---

*Determinism denies the existence of free choice or self-choice, whereas self-determinism suggests personal freedom which has no external decision making.

first one. All others are affected by previous choices and the particular choice will affect all the others. In this manner we create our own essence and mold our own choices.

Purpose

One way to talk about the effects of previous choices is to discuss the idea of purpose. Certainly a lot of human time and effort is expended in seeking the "purpose in life." We ask ourselves questions about why we are here—assuming as we do that our creation implies a reason or purpose. When early human beings were trying to scratch a life from barren soil they probably did not think a lot about why they were there. But when they found themselves with free time and could enjoy the luxury of thinking the idea of purpose arose. Over the years civilization has developed some hooks upon which to hang ideas about this purpose for life.

First of all we can look at purpose as focus.[2] One kind of focus concerns the consummation of the action. For example, when I watch one of the Kansas City Royals' baseballs players hitting the ball, I know that the purpose of the swing of the bat is to hit the ball.

However, much of what we do is designed not for the purpose of consummation but rather as a means to an end. For many persons, usually amateurs, the purpose behind the game is not hitting the ball but to get the exercise that accompanies playing the game. The first we can see is an action of consummation while the second is a means to an end.

Another purpose of the action may be in the action itself. For example, a person who enjoys playing baseball may not really have as her purpose either hitting the ball or getting exercise. She may simply enjoy being involved. Thus if one is looking at behavior in terms of being ethical, many would suggest that one's ethics depends a great deal on the purpose of the behavior just like it does the purpose of swinging the bat.

Another way to look at purpose within the context of freedom is to identify the restrictions imposed by the way we focus our expectations. This is a little harder to define but deals with purpose as idea or attitude. Such identification is often called "named purpose." The big four are: significance, work, aesthetics, and curiosity. Obviously there are many others but these will help make the point.[3]

1. The idea of a significant life leads us to try to live meaningfully (significantly) by accepting life as fully as we can. It requires making the most of life by finding, pehaps even making-up, a value and design for life itself. Some persons even feel a sense of destiny about their lives. Such a focus will define purpose within the framework of these values.

2. Work is used here, but the word *play* would be just as good. It speaks of the presence of something we want to do, or to accomplish. We focus on this accomplishment for many reasons but primarily because it "needs to be done." Academic types often have something they "are working on," meaning a statement or presentation which reflects the focus of their studies. They cannot always identify it, but they are often driven by the need to be doing it—doing their "own work." This is the work, the purpose of completion, the goal fulfilled. All of these needs limit the individual's freedom to do otherwise. For it haunts them as the Holy Grail haunted the hero in romance literature.

44

3. The term *aesthetics* suggests that purpose is found in the satisfaction of experiencing things outside of ourselves. It refers to the pursuit of experience and the search for untasted things. Life is to be lived, to be enjoyed, to be appreciated, allowing ourselves to be restricted only by the context rather than by the consequences.

CASE IN POINT. . . DOUBLE BIND[4]

The whole question of contradictions arises in ethics around what is called the "double bind." This bind illustrates how we often give rise to unsuspected problems while we think we are solving another set of problems. Follow these two lines of things:

"What is a free action?" (Question of Meaning)	"Is the belief in freedom compatible with the belief in universal causation?" (Question of Logical Relatedness)
"Is it the case that some actions are free?" (Question of Truth)	"Some actions are Free" (Basic Assumption of Criminal Justice)
"All actions are caused" (Basic Assumption of Science)	
Natural World	Personal Experience

—Confrontation about Cause—

Questions for Consideration

- How does the idea of free choice and universal causation conflict? If they do not, consider why they do not.
- Do we have personal experiences that suggest that everything is caused and at least partially determined by that which causes it?
- How can we understand criminal justice if we believe that all things are caused? If persons are not free in their actions how can we blame them?
- If some actions are free and some are caused, what is the cause of the difference?

4. The fourth is the focus of *disinterested curiosity*. This stance suggests that life is for testing, a proving ground for later life or future goals. Life searches for knowledge for its own sake; art and beauty are events not ends. This is the view that projects the purpose of human activity as educational and assumes knowing is all the purpose that one needs.

Another way to look at the relationship between purpose and choice is to recognize the extent to which purpose serves as a guide. We could identify several ways in which this is true but four are worth our consideration here: balance, friendship, love, and integrity. These are arbitrary, perhaps even exclusive, but they will help to see purpose as it imposes limitations on behavior.

1. In seeking balance we are pursuing harmony between what we know and what we do. We desire to make what we do responsive to the light of our knowledge. We are all aware how often our behavior appears to run counter to our actions. People

46

choose to smoke despite the U.S. Surgeon-General's warnings. One purpose, then, is the desire to bring unity between our knowledge and our actions.

2. The second purpose—friendship—reflects our desire to maintain meaningful harmony with our external groups, both personal and institutional. This reflects our necessary relationship with persons and groups to which we have no sense of commitment but for whom we recognize a sense of responsibility. This purpose is fulfilled as we harmonize our needs and wants with the persons and the communities with which we interact.

3. The third is love. In a more intense manner we seek this same harmony between ourselves and God. Through the centuries persons have manifested a concern for their relationship with an ultimate other. Christians have generally identified such a relationship with God. For the sake of our discussion it doesn't matter if this relationship is personal as in a love affair, or institutional as in a church relation, or to a divine presence. In each case persons are involved in trying to establish harmony between themselves as significant persons and that most significant other to which their lives and actions are directed.

4. A fourth harmony is often the most difficult of all. It is called integrity. This is the harmony we seek among the various aspects of our own self. It is the search for wholeness and personal peace. We all seem to be searching for a chance to ''be at peace.'' Our ultimate purpose is often ''to be at one with myself.'' One of the significant gaps in our generation, I am afraid, is the failure to recognize this feeling of incompleteness. This feeling may well be as much an ethical problem as it is a psychological

one. The harmony we seek in this purpose is the harmony of self-identity.

The Unethical

The failure to complete or move toward the fulfillment of these purposes is what we consider to be unethical. Our designated purposes are designed to direct human behavior. But also, in a negative manner, they aid in the identification of that which is considered unethical or immoral. To put it in the jargon of ethics: ''We choose wrongly when we choose in a way which is detrimental to the human goods (purposes) embodied in the options not chosen.''[5] When we say that an act is unethical or immoral, we tend to mean one of the following four things:

1. We mean the action is unreasonable. To say an act is immoral means it does not result in the harmony we seek between what we know to be true and what we are considering doing. The balance of this relationship is broken by the considered action, thus the action is declared unethical.

2. An act is unethical if it will do violence to the balance that may exist between the person and the eternal world in which he or she must live. It is a relationship, remember, in which a sense of commitment is restricted but one in which the idea of responsibility is valid. If one's action is going to cause difficulty in that world, then it is usually termed unethical.

3. Immorality is often used to mean an action or behavior breaks the commitment or tarnishes the relationship that exists between the actor and a significant other. It makes little difference if the relationship is with one's lover, church, or God.

48

4. Finally, it refers to a violation in which one is betraying personal integrity. The sign of this is guilt and the burden very heavy. "To do that would be to betray who I really am." Few talk like that anymore but the sentiment is valid. It is unethical (immoral) to do anything which violates who I really consider myself to be.[6]

Choosing

In order to complete this brief account of freedom and purpose, we should look at the idea of choice. There are three things which might be of help here.

1. First of all, choice implies that there is more than one solution. To really have a choice means that the human pressures which drove you to seek a choice were honest, that there really is more than one choice as well as more than one solution. In the very powerful story by William Saroyan, *Sophie's Choice,* we find a moving illustration of this point. While Sophie's choice between which of her young children would be allowed to live was a devastating one, it *was* a legitimate choice. To not have chosen, or to have chosen to strike the Nazi officer, would not have freed them both. She had more than one option and she chose.

2. Second, we have exclusive choice. There are choices which, when we make them, identify all other choices as being bad or irrelevant. Before the choice was made the options were open and every other choice had some validity (or they would not be chosen). After the exclusive choice the alternatives all lose their validity. The exclusiveness of the choice diverts the action or behavior to a limited or well-defined goal.

On the other hand, we have what are called inclusive choices. In this case the alternatives have not all been rejected, just not chosen. The options remain open and the choices are defended on the basis of their appropriateness, not of their exclusive value. Sophie's choice was inclusive.

3. Moral (ethical) choice usually refers to what we have chosen to do not to why we have chosen it. Many folks consider it ethical to "do what they have to do." It is not. That is *only* doing what you have to do. Ethical choice is choosing when you really have a choice, and when the choice is a reasonable (that is, reasoned-out) action.

Quiz

Identify which of the following are true or false according to this chapter on freedom and choice. Put T or F in the space provided.

_____ 1. Most persons have freedom as their goal.

_____ 2. Most persons feel controlled by environment.

_____ 3. Primary limitations come from the outside.

_____ 4. We are restricted by our expectations as well as our goals.

_____ 5. We can have ethics even if we do not have freedom.

_____ 6. Self-determination is a manner in which we mold ourselves through choice.

_____ 7. Every action has only one purpose.

_____ 8. Aesthetics is used to suggest that purpose is found from outside ourselves.

_____ 9. Ethical balance is seeking harmony between what we think and what we do.

_____ 10. Friendship is our desire to maintain harmony with external groups.

End Notes

1. Paul Edwards, "Hard and Soft Determinis" as quoted in William Frankena, and John Granrose, *Introductory Readings in Ethics* (New Jersey: Prentice-Hall, Inc., 1974), 275–282.
2. For a discussion of this idea see Russell Shaw, *Choosing Well* (Notre Dame: University of Notre Dame Press, 1982), 10–14. I am indebted to Russell Shaw both for raising the point and for aiding in the outlining of it here.
3. Again I am indebted to Russell Shaw for commentary on these "named purposes." *Choosing Well*, 10–14.
4. Based on an illustration in "Philosophical Attitudes" found in Mark Woodhouse, *A Preface to Philosophy* (Wadsworth Publishing Company: Belmont, California, 1984), 6.
5. *Choosing Well*, 40.
6. *Choosing Well*, 40–41.

CHAPTER 3

MEANS, INTENTIONS, AND ENDS

Any means is justified by the ends they accomplish.

—Machiavelli

Milo Guard was aware that the child needed the camping experience. Crippled as she was, the chance to spend several days in the open air with people of her own age and free from the limitations of always having to cope was just the sort of treatment needed. It only cost $150 and he had saved nearly $90 toward the amount. So when the unattentive customer left an envelope containing $75 on the counter where Milo worked, it seemed too good an opportunity to miss. The money was quickly brushed into his bag. The customer would never know and, he reasoned, would probably never miss it. The customer was too careless with money. The crippled child could spend a week at camp and all was well.

Sound familiar? You probably have never faced this particular problem but we have all dealt with similar temptation. The question is this: Is it okay (ethical) to commit an act which you would normally consider unethical in order to accomplish a good cause? Does the bishop's lie (in our story *Les Miserables*) become ethical because it saves a man from prison? Or, as we usually ask the question, does the end justify the means? The world's love for the Robin Hood myth is not just because we all like knights and yeomen with long bows. We find some sort of delight in taking from the rich and giving to the poor, and we can sympathize not only with the actions of Robin Hood but with the greater good that he is doing.

The problem, of course, goes further. What do we in a democracy do when persons stand up and speak against the democracy? Can we bridle their freedom of speech in order to preserve our freedom of speech? Is it ethical for the police officer to violate the law to uphold the law? For the minister to act immorally to save the church? These questions concern ends and means. Within the ethical community there is a warning that goes likes this: "Do not be lured into immoral behavior by the grand morality of that which it will produce."

On the other hand, as rational human beings we are well aware it is sometimes necessary to create pain in order to prevent it. The so-called "surgeon's knife" thesis explains this best. While the surgeon has no desire to hurt the patient nor does the patient desire to be hurt, both are aware that the pain involved in having the appendix removed is valid because of the consequences. Thus we believe the end (no appendix) does justify the means (the pain of cutting it out).

In this chapter we will be discussing some of the characteristics of ethical decisions and arguments. We will, therefore, look at the means of ethical action, consider intention in the field of ethics, as well as ambiguous actions, contracts, and covenants within ethical behavior, and the conflict of duties and ends.

Moral Responsibility

When we say persons are responsible we are generally saying one of three things. We mean (1) that they have the kind of character that allows them to see what has to be done, see that it is done, and not try and ignore it or push it off on someone else; (2) something has happened in the past and the reason it happened is directly related to the persons we have deemed responsible for it. They may or may not have caused it (that is, been the motivation) but it would not have happened if they had chosen that it not happen. Or (3) there is something in the future to be done and that the person who must see it done—or has accepted the role of seeing that it will be done—is the person we say is responsible for it.

If we are trying to identify moral responsibility then we will need to recognize that in the first case mentioned (character) and the third case (promise) we are considering implication but not application. That is, they are connected to the act but did not cause it. In the second case we are talking about a person being responsible for what has happened. And it is of value here to look at what this means. Many answers have been provided—as many as there are philosophies—but Aristotle made some points worth consideration. To say one is responsible is to suggest

- that he or she was *able* to commit the act and that in fact (in reality) he or she did commit the act.
- the cause of what was done came from within them; that it was not some outside force that could itself be blamed. It was not a case where "the devil made us do it."
- the decision to act was not made in ignorance.

54

- that the person could have done otherwise—that is, that he or she had a real choice.
- that it was possible to have chosen otherwise; that is, they were not so determined by habit or convention that any other choice was impossible.

To say someone is responsible, then, is to suggest he or she is directly and individually the factor which, because of this free action, allows or causes something to happen.

Intention

There is something within us that suggests our intentions are important. Maybe it is an urge for fair play or justice. We tend to accept the idea that what was intended by the actor is important to the outcome produced by the action. There is serious question, however, if this is true. We all understand the situation. Maybe we are driving and hit a parked car when the wheel seems to fly from our hands, or we cause a lot of discomfort for a person when we repeat a story they were not supposed to tell us. In either case what we did was not designed to bring harm, we did not intend to cause them any problem, nor did we consider the ethical nature of the act and decide to commit it regardless of the consequences.[2] Our intentions were good yet harm resulted. We are concerned about this enough that we support the idea "the streets of hell are paved with good intentions." Yet we must deal with the skeptic's response: "Therefore, the streets of heaven must be paved with bad intentions."

Within the study of ethics it is usually assumed persons are morally responsible for what they have chosen, and that persons cannot separate their behavior from what they believe. Ethics contends it

55

would be difficult to be loving persons and yet not love. Thus the implication is there, that persons do what they think or want or evaluate. Yet it seems there is a considerable difference between accepting something that is, and intending it be that way. It is not enough that we mean well, the expectation is that we *do* well.

I draw on an illustration from my youth when the most bizarre sort of action occurred. I was playing in the street as was the custom on North Delaware in Independence, Missouri, where I grew up. A car—a fairly rare event in those days—was coming down the street too fast. One of the smaller children, sort of hanging around the street rather than playing with us, was in danger of being hit. The child stood still and the driver, realizing the child was there, abruptly swung the car to its left to avoid hitting the child. One of the boys, somewhat older than myself, saw what was happening and ran toward the young child. In doing so he tripped. He plowed headlong into the smaller child and his momentum pushed the child into the area where the car, trying to avoid the child, had redirected its motion. The child was hit and killed.

No one would suggest that the intentions of the older boy were not good. They would agree his actions were based on what we all could identify as a "right" or "good" and his act—at least as far as running toward the child—would be beyond question. However, it is fairly obvious the young child would have been saved if he had not been "rescued" by the older boy. What role does the older boy's intentions play?

Within our discussion of intention there are four points to be considered. They concern personality, responsibility, acceptability, and intentionality. Let us look at them one at a time.

1. Someone has suggested if you do not do what you believe, you will soon believe what it is that you do. There is a lot of truth in this, as you know. It is important to remember, then, that much of the "who" and "what" that I am comes out of the intentions behind my act. If I am basically an unkind person then that personality becomes a kind of intention. My actions will express the sort of person that I am because—and this is the point—the kind of person that I am is a kind of habitual intention.

2. It is necessary also, in consideration of intentionality, to assume that I am responsible for what my intentions and behavior produce. When I take an action and understand that the outcome of the action will produce some harm, then I am intentionally doing harm. If this is not a case of responsibility then the intentionality probably is a question of cause rather than of ethics.

3. Russell Shaw, whose work *Choosing Well* has served as a general outline for much of this chapter, suggests that in considering the idea of intention we must recognize the difference between intending and accepting. It is an important distinction and can be illustrated easily. We do not intend the pain that results from having a bone set, but we do accept it as a part of the overall plan to heal a break.[3]

4. Our intentions are not the totality of our moral act. The intention in racing toward the child was to save the child. Even if we knew from experience that we would fail in the effort, can we *assume* the ethical goodness—the rightness—of the intention?

Ambiguous Actions

Unfortunately all ethical choices are not clear. The key to ethics is the fact that one has a choice, but it is important to remember that the difficulty of ethical judgment often arises because of the paradoxical or ambiguous nature of the options. It is quite often the case that right and wrong are joined together in the same action.

There are several ways we try to deal with the ambiguous situation. The most popular way is to ignore the problem. This is done fairly easily as we assume the more positive side of the action, accepting the negative side as a side effect. This allows the positive part of the good to override any consideration of the bad. On the opposite side of this assumption are those who state that bad in any form must be avoided even when it may (will) provide some other wanted good. Thus their simple answer is to suggest that no bad be done. They resolve the conflict by declaring that it is not one.

Relying on Russell Shaw again,[4] we find some other, and probably more helpful, responses to ambiguous situations.

1. If it is possible to bring about the good desired without bringing bad (damage) to that or any other good, then one should do it.

2. When the ambiguous action cannot be avoided, one should act in a manner that brings as little bad to the good as possible.

3. In those cases where the decision must be made quickly and without much thought, the role of intention becomes significant and should play an important—perhaps decisive—part.

4. Anticipating the ambiguous nature of ethics helps reduce the impact of the ambiguousness.

58

This is very interesting advice and is certainly better than no advice at all. But it does little to relieve the situation. The point is that much ethical action lies buried in the conflicts and ambiguousness of multiple actions. One of the very difficult aspects of human involvement is that persons very rarely sin (any more than they are saved) alone.

Conflict

Closely associated with the problem of ambiguity is the difficulty of conflict. Conflict arises from the challenge of obligations imposed by decisions one has already made, the commitments one has arranged, and the responsibilities that have been accepted. For the sake of clarification, the duties I speak of have been identified as promises and memberships.

1. Membership imposes duties. When we join something, or accept something which identifies us as members of a group or community, we succomb to a set of duties. These obligations emerge from the group's dependence on our willingness to represent it fairly. The group depends on the right to count on us and to assume our responsibility toward it. These duties are not in themselves moral obligations, but the fact they are promises may well impose moral obligations. Becoming a member of the church imposes on us such obligations and responsibilities. They stem from the advantages we enjoy and from the rights of other members who share the name with us.

2. Promises are contracts. They concern duty which arises from agreements we make with persons and institutions. These promises are statements about future behavior and are commitments

on which other persons base their decision-making. When we promise to cut the grass, we are saying that the one to whom we made the promise can proceed with the assurance the grass will be cut. To break this promise is to violate an expectation and, in effect, to alter the environment in which others are making their own decisions.

The American Constitution, for example, makes this promise when it states that no laws can be passed that make you guilty (*ex post facto*). Suppose you parked your car on the side street next to your office yesterday. A law passed today, making it illegal to park your car in that spot—effective yesterday—would make you guilty without you having the chance to choose not to commit the crime. The law, according to the Constitution, can only alter the future. It can never violate the foundation of past decision-making.

Conflict emerges when a promise or a membership commitment challenges action that might otherwise be taken. The most obvious confrontation is when duties imposed by a promise interfere with obligations imposed by membership. This is the conflict between institutions and personal wants, between church and state, between love and country. Richard Lovelace's romantic "answer" is an indication of the conflict as it affects us personally: "I could not love thee half as much loved I not honor more."

In such conflicts we are often faced with the identification of *primary* ethical obligations. "Render unto Caesar those things which are Caesar's and to God those things which are God's." If that were the case it would be fairly simple. The conflict arises when Caesar and God seem to want the same thing.

60

I am reminded here of an experience I had some years ago while being sworn into the military. I was only nineteen years old but even then was aware of the paradox. I was in a room full of persons standing in their crumpled civilian clothes with their hands in the air. A military chaplain from Kansas City stood in front having us swear to God that we would kill on command. If I were willing to break God's commandment ("Thou shalt not kill"), why did anyone feel I would not just as easily break my promise to God to kill when ordered? Besides, after having made such a commitment, having sworn such a loyalty to those placed over me by my society, what was my option when it came time to pull the trigger?

When we faced the trials after World War II, the American people seemed appalled at the fact that Nazi officers and soldiers performed atrocities on the basis of simply following orders. It is not wise to assume that one has a moral obligation to obey every law, to accept every unwise social system; but it is not wise either to assume that every individual must be the judge of whether to obey the law or not.

E. F. Carritt suggests that for most of us conflicts can be solved by the realization that ethical choices which appear to be in conflict usually are not. His point is that in most cases when ethical convictions are compared, one can see that one action is *obviously* superior. When that happens there is no conflict, only degrees of expectation. They are then more like the ambiguous assumptions we noted earlier.[5]

Ends

The complication of human efforts toward values

can be more easily understood by looking at a simple exercise adapted from Richard L. Portill.[6] It assumes that we can identify what seems valuable to us. If we identify these by the letter *B to mean bad and by G to mean good,* then we can symbolize the various value levels by using the following:

B means bad for others

G means valuable for others

b means bad for ourselves

g means valuable for ourselves

This provides us with several ways to identify behavior:

1. g = G: Doing something good for oneself in order to bring about good for others. For example, cooking (which you love) in order to provide meals for those who cannot provide meals for themselves.

2. b = G: Doing something bad for oneself in order to accomplish something good for others. For example, willingness to drive persons to work even at your expense and inconvenience because they need to go to work.

3. g = B: Doing something good for oneself in order to bring about bad for others. For example, refusing to use your car to take persons to work thus saving time and money for yourself but resulting in their loss of jobs.

4. b = B: Doing something bad for oneself in order to bring about bad for others. An example would be letting the air out of your tires to be sure you can't take them to work.

5. G = g: Doing something good for others in order to bring about good for yourself. An example would be cooking which you enjoy for those to whom eating your meals is a pleasure.
6. B = g: Doing something bad for others in order to bring about good for yourself. Stealing food and having a party of your own for only your friends.
7. G = b: Doing something good for others in order to bring about bad for yourself. An example would be to take them all out to eat, paying the bill at considerable cost especially when you are on a diet.
8. B = b: Doing something bad for others in order to bring about something bad for yourself. Continue to steal food from the group even though they know it, have called the police, and need only one more bit of evidence.

In terms of our behavior we are inclined to identify these with terms as:
   1. Decent behavior
   2. Altruistic behavior
   3. Malicious behavior
   4. Spiteful behavior
   5. Self-serving behavior
   6. Selfish behavior
   7. Self-torturing behavior
   8. Self-destructive behavior

Contracts and Covenants

Part of the difficulty we all have with ethics is that it is not a science. It would be so much easier if there were formulas that would apply to given situations. But there are no formulas to be applied wherever we wish. Ethics is also very much an attitude as well as action, and this is hard to define. Perhaps the most formulized aspect is our concern about means and ends which revolve around the distinction between contracts and covenants. What seems to be the problem is that many people are making covenants and responding to contracts or making contracts and expecting covenants.

A contract is an agreement which states what each will do in a given situation. While there will be some flexibility, of course, it is, nevertheless, true that when those situations change the contract is violated. Persons who make contracts are often very careful to make sure it covers every contingency. And we hire lawyers to be sure there are no loopholes. As long as you "keep your end of the contract" things are okay, presuming, of course, that I keep my end of the contract. We make a contract to assure each other of future behavior, of actions that serve our best interests and accomplish our purposes. The contract binds us to the best considerations we both have at the moment. It is our guarantee we can count on one another in a given situation.

A covenant, however, is an agreement—almost a commitment— through which we bind ourselves to the purpose of our union. The covenant ties us to behavior now, and in the future, based on the expectations of our mutual advantage. A convenant agreement between two partners may well go beyond whatever contract binds them. It is based on what we feel committed to. It is not dependent on the environment or the situation when it was made as much as it does on the continuing nature of the relationship. True, in a covenant persons may breach the contractual nature of the agreement. But because of the mutual desire that it continue, they keep that goal in mind. Thus the goal is more important than the details of the agreement. It is a spiritual attachment or association not a legal one.

Obviously many human relationships tend to respond better to covenants than to contracts. Marriage, I would hope, is more a covenant than a contract. Obviously things are not the same after twenty-five years of marriage as they were when the marriage first took place. But the fact that the marriage reflects a commitment mutually made, keeps it meaningful even if the operating basis of the union has been broken and replaced.

A part of the ethical conflict and ambiguity persons face lies in the question of whether their relationships are contractual or covenantal.

Beginnings

In this book it is my intention to investigate some of the more significant ethical difficulties, as well as some areas in which others have claimed to have found solutions. Before doing that, and in preparation for further inquiry, it might be wise to make some very brief and simplified comments about ethics. Where do we begin? What are the options? Against what criteria do we choose? Rather than provide a set of formal definitions and ''isms'' about which we might later discuss, it seems appropriate here to suggest some ways of thinking about ethics. Where do the rules come from? Against what are they challenged? Who is responsible? How are such rules defended? Let me suggest five responses all based on the general idea of source.

Sources

1. Many ethical questions and responses are based on the assumptions that an *act*—that is a given behavioral event—is the source of the answer. It is the act that is the major problem. Over the years this has been generally true of such things as murder or illicit sex. It is the *act* of murder we see as wrong. In the act of performing those things a moral reality is violated, and thus it is unethical or immoral.

2. A seemingly opposite point of view is the idea of *rule* ethics. Rule ethics suggests there is a rule—usually coming from some outside or cosmic source—against which acts are measured. Is there a rule against this? If so, do not do it. If there is no rule against it then it can be done. It is not so much the act of murder that is wrong, as it is the violation of the rule against murder which is wrong. Strict constructionists would say if there is no rule in favor, it must not be done. Loose constructionists would be happy just to discover that there is no rule against it, then they would feel free to be involved.

3. A third source to be mentioned is *situational*. This view is not to be confused with situational ethics, for it acknowledges that it is the given situation which is the determining factor. The conditions under which the act is performed—that is, the time, the place, the frame of mind, the intention—are all a part of this decision. Rather than judge a given act or respond to a stated rule, one must rather react to the situation—unique as it will be—with a unique response.

4. A fourth and related idea is called conceptual

or *consequential*. This term suggests the ethics of an action (behavior) rests in the consequence of what is done. Neither the act itself nor any rule about it is a valid judge of the right or wrong. Nor does it depend on the situation in which the action is taken. Rather, right or wrong depends on the outcome, the consequence. If the outcome is good then the action is good.

5. A fifth source is called *contextual*—that is, in the larger or relative situation. Contextual ethics is the suggestion that the environment of an ethical situation is the primary source of information about its rightness or goodness. Culture, history, racial background, or even occupational considerations play the part of identifying "correct" behavior in this relativistic point of view. Doing what the Romans do—when in Rome—may be the best ethical response.

6. Finally, what is called *subjective* ethics identifies the source of ethical decision-making as the individual who is making the choice. It is, they say, a matter of strictly individual decision. This decision is attached to no act, no rule, no context, no situation; it is based on the assumption that whatever an individual person decides to do, is right. In a strict sense, of course, this is not an ethic. It is not an ethic because ethics, by definition, is involved in identifying moral truths and principles of conduct, and this does not. However, it is the basis for a lot of ethical decision and, to some degree, ethical systems.

Quiz

Identify if the following questions from chapter 3 are true or false, *according to the author*, by placing a T or an F in the place provided.

____ 1. To say we are responsible means we are able to commit or not commit an action.

____ 2. If you do not do what you think, you will soon think as you do.

____ 3. There is a difference between intending and accepting.

____ 4. An ambiguous action is both good and bad.

____ 5. Persons rarely sin, or are saved, alone.

____ 6. Membership in an organization imposes no duties to that organization.

____ 7. Promises depend on the circumstances and are not contracts.

____ 8. E. F. Carritt says conflict in ethics exists only because we do not recognize priorities in ethical claims.

____ 9. A covenant is the same as a contract.

____10. A consequential ethic is the same as a situational one.

End Notes

1. "Social Justice and Equal Access to Health Care," *Journal of Religious Ethics*, Vol. 2, No. 1, 1974, p. 11–29.
2. William K. Frankena, *Ethics*, Second Edition (Englewood Cliffs, New Jersey: Prentice Hall, Inc., 1963), 71–73.
3. Russell Shaw, *Choosing Well* (London: University of Notre Dame Press, 1982).
4. Ibid., 66–68.
5. E. F. Carritt, *The Theory of Morals* (Oxford: The Clarendon Press, 1928) as quoted in William Frankena and John Granrose *Introductory Readings in Ethics* (New Jersey: Prentice-Hall, Inc., 1974), 69.
6. *Thinking About Ethics* (New Jersey: Prentice-Hall, Inc., 1976), 20–21.

CASE IN POINT . . . THE LARGER COMMUNITY

During World War II American forces fighting in North Africa in 1943 discovered they were desperately short of medical supplies, particularly penicillin. There were two groups who could benefit most from the drug: those with infected battle wounds and those with venereal disease. It was the decision of the authorities the drug should go to those with VD. The reasoning was simple: those with wounds might well recover but not enough to go back into the battle where they were needed. Those with VD would recover and be available to fight and would cut out the spread of the disease.

Gene Outka[1] suggests that American society has developed five concepts of social equality. They are

1. To each according to merit or desert; that is, care should be given to those who have paid their way, made a contribution, or who need to be rewarded by the society.
2. To each according to one's societal contribution, rewarding for the greatest contribution to the largest number.
3. To each according to one's ability to satisfy that desired by others—that is, care on the supply-and-demand basis; those who can pay should be cared for.
4. To each according to a need based on a standard that all accept. Standard service must be provided. The standard is a political as well as a medical or ethical limit.
5. Similar treatment for similar cases, concluding that there are no cases under which arbitrary treatment is justified. All persons should have equal access as needed to the whole spectrum of health services.

Questions for Consideration

- Are these consistent with each other?
- What is the underlying assumption of the military decision on VD?
- Reflect on the question: ''Does the end justify the means'' as it relates to the above?

CHAPTER 4

RULES, ACTS, AND OBLIGATIONS

It is easier to do one's duty to others than to one's self.

If you do your duties to others, you are considered reliable.

If you do your duty to yourself, you are considered selfish.

—Thomas Szasa

Suppose you are sitting quietly on a park bench just before evening. A well-dressed man walks down the sidewalk toward you. He is carrying a long narrow package slightly smaller than your forearm. The man passes, then stops and turns toward you.

''Are you going to be sitting here awhile?'' he asks.

''Yes,'' you reply not really knowing how to respond.

He begins to talk and for about an hour the two of you have an interesting and pleasant conversation. He is obviously an intelligent and well-informed person as well as being personable. Again he asks you if you will be at the bench for a while and again you tell him you will.

Then he asks, ''You seem like an honest person, can I trust you?''

After a moment's hesitation you assure him that you are indeed honest and that he can trust you.

"Then," he said, "may I leave this package with you?" He pauses. "And will you promise to give it back to me when I return in just a few minutes?"

"Yes, certainly," you promise. What can be the harm in this? "I will be happy to keep it for you and to return it to you when you get back. Just as long as you do so before dark when I must leave."

"Thank you," he says handing you the package. "I appreciate this." He smiles. "You see my ex-wife walks this way on her way home just before dark. I intend to meet her here and kill her. The knife I am going to use is in the package and I am relying on you to let me have it when I get back." He then wanders off.

Recognizing that this is farfetched (but not so much as you might wish) it illustrates some ethical problems. The practical question is "Do I give the knife back as I promised when he returns?" Associated with that are many other questions: "Do I call the police?" "Do I put the knife down on the bench and run?" "Do I warn the ex-wife?" "Do I keep my promise?"

Such a quandary provides the basis for unlimited discussion of ethical theory. Let me identify just a few:

- There would appear to be a clash between consequences and rules (always keeping a promise *versus* helping this man kill his ex-wife).
- A hierarchy of values (Is killing worse than breaking a promise?).
- Some questions about particular rules versus universal or general rules. Is this a particular situation in which the general rules do not work or a general situation in which particular decisions would be unethical?

- The question of relative associations (Do the rights of the ex-wife overrule the rights of the man?).
- Do ethical rules have exceptions? Do exceptions exist? If so, when and under what situations, as well as how might we know when those exceptions exist?

The first step in deciding what to do, however, is not necessarily the quest for ethical guidance. Rather, one should begin by seeking further general knowledge and/or greater clarity. It is often the case that persons would be clear about what they should do if they understood what was involved. Our primary need then, as William Frankena is quoted as saying, is to avoid "our ready acquiescence in unclarity and our compliance in ignorance."[1]

Once we feel sure of the factual nature of our consideration, then there are two additional concepts within Western philosophy's tradition of normative ethics. The first of these is called *teleological* (sometimes called consequential), and the second called *deontological* or formal ethics. In short, the first can be identified as the ethical system in which the rightness or wrongness of action or event is determined by the results produced. If I shoot an arrow in the air and it falls harmlessly to the ground then there is no problem; if it hits a police officer, then it is evil. The second theory, deontological, holds that the rightness or wrongness of an act is determined through an examination of the act itself, the motives which led to the act, or perhaps even rules pertaining to such actions.

Consequences

The teleological view suggests an ethical position based on the tendency of the action to produce

73

good or bad consequences. Will returning the knife to the friendly stranger accomplish something you—and he—would consider good? It is not basically concerned with rules or descriptions of the action but rather with the consequences. The act is determined to be "good" if the consequences of the act produce more good than evil.

In the case of the friendly knifer, the proper behavior would not be to check such actions against any rules or laws of the society. Nor would it rest in the inherent goodness or badness of any of the many acts you might well perform. There is nothing inherently evil or unethical in returning a knife. Returning the knife would free you as well from any ultimate answers concerning promises or lying. The answer lies exclusively in the consequences of your act. If it can be determined that the consequence of your act will promote acceptable goals for human beings (the ex-wife lives, the man is not a murderer, the ex-wife has a disease which—if allowed to continue—will kill all humans—or some such answer) then it is ethical. Because the consequences here are personal, the personal goals will be more primary than any social ones.

The teleological view does not become an ethic of identifiable rules, laws, or inherent events, but rather of norms. A world of saintly persons who seek valid consequences is better than a world of strong-minded religious legalists who would never break or violate a rule. Nothing is clear-cut; we are seeking *individual* actions which lead to a good or to an ultimately good condition.

Confusion easily might emerge from this position. It seems what many call *norms* are really rules. If the ultimate good of the society is for its citizens *never to lie,* then what starts out to be an ethic of consequences appears to become an ethic of rule. The difference is that the teleological position identifies the norms as standards. These norms are not universal truths but have a sort of hierarchy emerging from experience. They could be identified as the following:

- *Conscientiousness* is a norm of morality. It is uniquely so in that it has as its end, morality itself; that is, keeping of moral rules. According to this ethical assumption every decision is made with the idea in mind to be moral. The desire to *be good* is the single consequence that is to be sought from all behavior.[2]
- *Principles* consist of basic assumptions about what it means to be good. It does not propose specific acts or identify specific actions that a person should undertake, but rather is a general guide to be used in the determination of behavior. Principles are not to be confused with a rule which would require obedience regardless of the outcome.
- *Rules* specify behavior and are not open to interpretation. The ethical rules would identify exactly what one would be expected to do and any exceptions that might exist.
- *Values* express the worth in a principle or rule. In effect such statements of value provide evidence that a given rule or principle is good.
- *Rights* suggest something that is due to persons by virtue of their personhood. Neither a rule nor a value, rights are expressed as a fact or as a matter of knowledge which, if one knows, surely must be taken into consideration on every account.
- *Virtues* express personal qualifications which are

deemed to be good. They identify actions or behaviors that would express the personal qualities seen as valid.

Duty and Obligations

What is called deontological ethics are principles in which action is determined to be right or wrong on the basis of a rule, a habit, or a command. This is an external principle based on a universal right rather than on the basis of the consequence of such an action. Again, in reference to our illustration, if the rule says "do not break your promise" then the ethical thing to do is to return the knife.

In this frame of reference all consequences are irrelevant to the rightness or wrongness of an action. Put more distinctly: We ought to do X because there is a rule that says that X should be done. This view also includes the possibility for a rule or behavior to be morally right even if the consequences produce a situation which we would consider bad.

The moral reasoning modeled by Socrates is based on references to a general rule taken as a premise on which to deduce the conclusion. All societies use public morality as the glue to hold the society together.

Act—Deontological Ethics

This aspect of ethical inquiry suggests moral decisions are all purely particular. It most often assumes that general rules can be developed for particular cases, but such a general rule can never exceed the particular judgments. This concept, best found in what is called situational ethics, offers no real standards or rules to judge against the process of trying to determine what is right and wrong. The method of making this determination identifies as clearly as possible what is involved and then, based on that clarity, a decision is made. It is the making of the decision which primarily validates the action.

These particular decisions are made on the basis of either an intuitive experience or an existential crisis. The intuitive decision is based on the feelings where one is "impressed" or "presented" the understanding of correctness. While this is logically a weak argument, it is not necessarily a bad one. Logically, it faces all the problems inherent in the metaphysical approach: How do you finally know? How can you tell this experience from stomach gas or any of hundreds of difficult understandings? What it generally means is that the decision is based on the feeling of coherence—what is sometimes called closure—that reflects humans' ability to accept information, codify it, present it, and deal with it in terms of the whole even if they cannot really describe how this is accomplished.

Existential acts/deontological decisions are those that take the situation as the guide and bring into it the ingredient of necessary choice. The existentialists recognize the need to choose and the realization that the nature of the choice may be less significant than the fact of the choice. In the case of our "friendly knifer," simply sitting on the park bench or leaving the park becomes a choice. To make a choice—even in the face of poor information and little understanding—is characteristic of the self-actualized person. The hard facts of this decision are that we must make a choice. Not to make a choice is a choice. To realize that and act accordingly—and then to live with the decision—is the existential act: being today the most directive and

77

controlling person over your own life as is possible.

The argument for each of these, of course, is not complete. There are many who will find fault with this view of ethics. The point for us to understand is that this view of ethics is based on the assumption—held strongly by many persons—that the situation is unique and dictates the response as much as any general rule could do. They are willing to develop rules (or standards) based on particular experience but never, under any circumstances, can the general rule take precedence over the particular understanding of ethical behavior.

Rule-Deontological Ethics

When we are called upon to choose we are implicitly selecting rules or principles—at least according to rule-deontologists. The rules become significant when one recognizes the situation which produces them. Certainly there are exceptions to the rules, but the exceptions result from the variations of the situation. Thus right or wrong consists of one or more rules of behavior. The rules are either concrete ones like "We must never tell a lie" or much more abstract principles like Kant's universals. These rules are considered to be valid even if they produce evil consequences. A rule like "Always tell the truth" must be followed even if someone is asking: "Where are the children so that I can sell them into slavery?" Obviously such a system makes its followers powerful defenders of the essential goodness (correctness) of the rule itself. These persons would wait on the park bench to return the knife. We will discuss the nature of the rules themselves later. Here we need only to recognize the ethical principle of *obedience of the rule* as the basis for behavior. When (if) one knows the rules, then one knows exactly what to do.[3]

Exceptions

Earlier we mentioned there were bound to be exceptions to the rules. No rule can be framed so well that it is always free of any situation where the rule does not apply. If this is true, and it certainly seems that it is, this would be a less extreme understanding and would suggest that rules may well become standards which are played off against each other. For example, the rule "Always tell the truth" may need to be matched against the rule "Never kill a person." This may well be true in the illustration at the beginning of the chapter. At least we would weigh them against each other. When these two are in conflict, it is obvious that most of us would judge the rule against murder to be of higher authority (because of its better source) than the one against not telling the truth. The person seeking an ethic may well find fault with this, feeling that if indeed rules are in conflict then no rule is universal. There are several ways of dealing with this.

One is the suggestion that an exception to a rule is, in effect, acknowledging another rule and allowing it to take precedence over the first rule. While the circumstances may suggest conflicting rules, what is really happening is that we recognize the value of one rule over the other. The answer is not that "there is an exception to the rule about always telling the truth" but rather that "the exception is an indication that another rule is coming into play."

The second point of view is that laws with exceptions are still laws. We tend to think of universals as if they were universally complete packages. For example, when asked about telling a lie we might indicate that it is bad except when it is done to save a person's life. The question then would be raised if it is indeed a universal law if it has an exception. When the exception is raised, however, it is not a violation of the universal but the description of the universal. Let me illustrate it in a somewhat simpler manner. When the rule says: "No parking except after 6:00 p.m." the "except after 6:00 p.m." is not an exception to the universal law "no parking." It is another universal law. And it is just as universal as saying no parking at all. It is, however, another universal. Thus to say "No lying except to save children" is just as universal as "No lying."

The viewing of the recent movie *Platoon* brings to mind again the difficulty of a world society in which persons grant blind obedience to authority. Within our generation we continue to deal with the German war machine under Hitler and its unethical behavior and have added the My-Lai incident in Vietnam. In each case we are asking about our own obedience problems. The willingness to behave in such a fashion reflects not only our lack of concern over any kind of individual responsibility, but also reflects our increasing sense of relativism where old standards seem either too simplistic or inadequate for our task. Or we begin to believe that there is no standard at all.

The traditional response of education and the church has not been very effective. Educators have been reasserting that it is not their business to teach values, or to give in to the wishes of the minority who seem to want religious instructions. Lately we find some social scientists asserting that you cannot teach persons to think or reason. The logic of that, of course, makes us wonder about the social scientist thinking and reasoning, but it is indicative of the relativism that sweeps society. And, whether by design or accident, schools and churches have become more and more happy to support a valueless society under the umbrella of not wishing to promote a particular value. Through what is sometimes called values clarification, the education system has recognized an ethic which traditionally has been called ethical egoism.

CASE IN POINT . . . KILLING

Consider for a moment the famous case of the ''innocent fat man.'' The fat man, a guide, was leading a group of persons out of a deep cave near the ocean when he became stuck at the mouth of the cave. High tide was upon them and unless he was freed, the water, rising from the inside, would drown them all. The only person who would be saved would be the fat man whose head was stuck out above the water level. As fate would have it one of the luckless tourists had a stick of dynamite with her and knew that she could easily blow the fat man out of the mouth of the cave. The only difficulty being that it would most certainly cause his death. The Christian would tend to say that killing is wrong—and that fact is true in every case—but there are a group of fine folks there just as innocent as the fat man. The issue is not to prevent death because a death will occur; the question is, whose?

The purist says that killing for any reason is bad. Yet others will say that there are circumstances when such violence must be ''reluctantly assented

81

to'' and in fact some cases when we are morally obligated to take a life.

Questions for Consideration

- If preventing death is not the issue in this story, what is?
- Is one death better—that is, less bad—than several deaths? Why?
- If one person must die does it matter who it is?
- If you suspect you would ''blow up the fat man'' like many would, what is the ''more important'' value that you are responding to?

CASE IN POINT . . . SELECTIVE KILLING

Consider the ''plain woman syndrome.'' There are two women on a lifeboat. One of these is a very plain woman, a housewife and mother who at age fifty-five is more an observer of history than a maker. With her on the boat is another woman, about 50, who knows that given a few more months she will be able to complete tests on a drug that will prevent the spread of the disease AIDS. It is determined by each that the boat will not carry both of them, nor will there be enough food or water to keep them both alive during the time necessary to reach safety. Should the scientist protect her life—and thus the lives of many others—by throwing the generally average housewife out of the boat?

Questions for Consideration

- Is it ever right to sacrifice an innocent person for the sake of an ideal?
- Is there a difference between the plain woman

82

throwing herself out into the sea to drown, and her being thrown out, as long as the decision is made on the basis of a good cause they both agree upon?

- What is the value of a community good versus an individual good?
- Do you see a difference here between this story and what we would call a ''hero''? What ethical principle is involved in your answer?

Quiz

Complete the following by placing the letter in the space provided that best completes the sentence.

1. The first step is to avoid _____.
2. The view that ethics is determined by the event's production of right or wrong is called

   _____.
3. Specific ethical behavior not open to inter-pretation or exception is called _____.
4. Due persons by virtue of their humanity: _____.
5. Actions determined to be right or wrong based on a rule are known as _____.
6. Teleogical ethics is sometimes called _____.
7. The norm of morality is called _____.
8. The basic assumptions about what it means to be good are called _____.

a. teleological
b. rights
c. consequential
d. ready acquiescence in unclarity

e. rules
f. deontological ethics
g. conscientiousness
h. values
i. ethical principles

End Notes

1. William K. Frankena, *Ethics* (New Jersey: Prentice-Hall, Inc. 1973), 13.
2. For a discussion of this see A. Campbell Garnett "Conscience and Conscientiousness" as found in William K. Frankena and John Granrose, *Introductory Readings in Ethics* (New Jersey: Prentice-Hall, Inc., 1974), 249-261.
3. William K. Frankena, *Ethics* (New Jersey: Prentice-Hall, Inc., 1973), 25-26.

CHAPTER 5

META-ETHICS AND THE SEARCH FOR A GENERAL PRINCIPLE

*I am an idealist. I don't know where I'm going,
but I'm on my way.*
—Carl Sandburg

Every dogma has its day, but ideals are eternal.
—Israel Zangwill

As if it isn't difficult enough to decide to be good, somewhere along the line most of us have tried to understand what a concept like "good" really means. Meta-ethics, as was mentioned in an earlier chapter, is the study of ethical principles. This part of ethical consideration asks questions about the meaning of concepts. And, perhaps even more importantly, asks if ethical judgments can be proven. As well, meta-ethics is concerned about identifying its source of ethical truth. In this chapter we will address the logical problem of ethical truths and then will deal with four concepts of justification: definist, noncognitive, intuitionism, and relativism.

Nominalism and Realism

Underlying all ethical rules and obligations is an inquiry into the assumptions of reality. The traditional way to approach the question is known by the terms *nominalism* and *realism.* The view that

85

the class of something—humankind for example—is only a name and has no reality of its own is called nominalism. This view says there is no such thing as humankind—the word refers only to a common name—only a vast number of persons who collectively are called human.

The opposing view is that the term humankind is the reflection of true reality. This suggests that humankind is the reality and that individual persons are particular examples or shadows of it. This is called realism.

There are many examples of this we could identify. When we use a term like cup, do we refer to the reality of the primary *cup* of which there are many copies, or particular examples? Being a dedicated coffee drinker, I have run into a lot of "things" from which to drink my coffee. In the course of a week (kept track for purposes of an illustration), I drank from a china cup, a mug, a paper cup, a saucer, a tin cup, a wax cup (ugh), a Styrofoam cup, a glass, a plastic cup, and the top of a thermos bottle. All of these looked, felt, tasted, smelled, and sounded different. Yet they were all cups. The realist would say that the primary reality of "cup" is whatever all of those things had in common—cupness. The nominalist would say the word cup is simply a word to simplify discussing all these containers. When you ask for a cup of coffee, are you asking for a *cup* of something, or something with "cupness"?

These questions may seem far-fetched to many and in most cases have little or no appeal for our consideration. But they do apply to us and to our study. For example, the difference in belief about priesthood calling in contemporary Protestant
86

churches is a reflection of this debate. The RLDS come down heavily,[1] but not exclusively, on the realistic side with the assumption that priesthood exists independently of those persons who hold it. If all the priesthood members in the world suddenly died there would still be priesthood because God is alive. Through individual callings persons share in priesthood. The RLDS tend to assume the same thing is true of authority. On the other hand, some Protestant groups take a very nominalistic view of priesthood. They hold that priesthood is the name given to a collection of persons, each of whom claims priesthood and who collectively have some joint characteristics.

Getting back to our question of ethics, we can see how these two views can be applied to rules or principles as well. Nominalism says that law, for example, is only a name for a lot of individual opinions agreed upon. Realism would identify law as being objective and independently real. Individual opinions are but particular examples, maybe even copies, of the real law. The same would be true for ethical principles. Nominalism would say an ethical principle ("Do not steal") is simply a description of ethical decisions made for other reasons. While realism would say the ethical principle ("Do not steal") is true and we simply copy it or build variations on it.

Thus the ethicists can ask: "Is God good because he is God, or is 'good' what God does?" Think about this. It makes a lot of difference to human behavior. Is there is "good"—objective and independent—that we are seeking? Or is "good" the name that we give to individual efforts which, when we see them collectively, we like. We tend to

87

be willing to say that beauty is in the eye of the beholder; do we believe the same about goodness?

Logic of Ethics

For many persons truth is rooted in empirical data. Empirical data is that data gathered by the senses. We tend to be informed by our senses in everyday events and determine the truth of something by these same senses. We then take this basic information and reason about it to determine if what is being said is correct in our minds. When a used car dealer tells you a car is "just like new and it has only been driven 5,000 miles" you may find that hard to believe. The car is ten years old, the upholstery is worn, the engine is dirty, the tires are bald, and the speedometer is broken. From what you can see, the truth of the dealer's statement does not coincide with the empirical evidence.

This way of determining truth is used by many persons and it provides them with a source of security about such things. Because they trust their senses they tend to use the same method in seeking answers about things less open to understanding by the senses. This process is called the "empirical fallacy." It occurs when we try to use empirical evidence to justify non-empirical things. It is our tendency to want ethical values to be rooted in some hard facts. If, however, we are not able to know in this fashion, then we seek to know by understanding, or by some sort of revealed or inherited truth.

If ethical principles are neither empirical nor revealed it is easy to assume that ethical value is arbitrary or relative. And we tend to push very hard to get "facts" about value. It is important to remember, however, that factual information is not necessarily information about values, nor is it wise to conclude that because we are able to do something that we are obligated to do it. The fact that blue and yellow make green is neither good nor bad, only a fact. And the fact that nuclear bombs *can* be manufactured does not mean that we are under an obligation—that we ought—to manufacture them.

Thus we need to ask if either our basic ethical positions or our value premises can be described logically from factual information. Can answers about "ought" and "good" be arrived at from a set of premises that do not include ought or good? The answer is "logically no." The rules of logic do not allow us to make a jump from one premise to another without a connecting premise. For example the following sounds like it makes sense: hitting your sister is injurious; thus, hitting your sister is bad. But it really tells us nothing. What is missing is the connection between injury and bad. Most of us would agree that hitting one's sister is bad, but that is not the point. The point is that logically the statement does not prove anything. If we said "Jumping up and down causes muscles" thus "jumping up and down is bad," you would ask, "What is the connection between muscles and bad?"

The way to connect these logically is to accept "injury is bad," as your second premise. The reason we cannot simply insert this second premise, as you can see, is because we would be begging the question. If we already know that injury is bad, then we already know the value. In any case we do not prove it logically.

In what is called the "rules of inference" the connection between the premise and conclusion is often made by implication. We say "hitting your sister causes injury" and thus "hitting your sister is bad"; we are implying we have already construed without logical reasoning that injury is bad.

Major premise: Hitting your sister causes injury.
Implied premise: (injury is bad)
Conclusion: Hitting your sister is bad.

This is little more than sugar coating an established principle, but it does explain the way much ethical "reasoning" is conducted.

Understand, please, this is not a suggestion about the truth or falsity of hitting someone, or whether that is bad. It is about logic. What we are looking at here is the reason why persons can say that ethical values are not arrived at logically. That is, you cannot prove an ethical value.

Definist

Persons who hold to the definist view of ethics also call themselves naturalists because their justification of ethical principles is rooted in the nature of things. In this ethical view terms like good or right are understood by what is *ordinarily* meant by the words. Good, for example, means an object of desire. Such a definition can be justified by identifying what we are calling good and checking to see if we desire it. These folks believe *ethical terms* stand for properties of things like good, and that *ethical statements* (principles) attach these properties to things. That is, we can attach good (meaning an object of desire) to honesty and thus determine that being honest is desirable.

Therefore, in a general way, they believe it is possible for ethical statements to be justified by
90

empirical inquiry just as any scientific or factual statement could be. They would argue that what we have identified as the "empirical fallacy" is no fallacy at all. They are aware there are many variations on the definitions of words used as ethical principles. But these have a common meaning which is the ethical core. The variations are alternative vocabulary for reporting the fact.[2]

Equally important is the definist view that "ought" can be defined in terms of "is." For example, if you define good as being the object of desire then any evaluation of "ought" is justified on the grounds that it is desired. If something is good then I ought to desire it. The notion of obligation (ought) seems to be a Judeo-Christian contribution to Greek morality, holding that *ought* is the core of moral discourse. This tradition says ought is commanded by God (by virtue of creation) or is at least in the natural order of things. Accepting that this is true, the definists say ethical terms can be defined in the same manner as unethical (factual) ones. When informative or factual statements include the word "ought" we are then justified in accepting them as ethical statements. "We *ought* to be good" needs to be accepted in the same manner we would accept "gravity makes things appear heavy." Thus the good tells us that we desire and the ought tells us that whatever we desire should be done. The problem of justification is not solved by appealing to a definition, however, for the description would then need to be justified, and so on *reducto ad absurdism.*

Intuitionism

The intuitionist position is sometimes called

91

"non-naturalistic" because it suggests other than natural sources of ethical understanding. It stands in opposition to the definists. Ethics does not and, in fact, cannot rest on logical assertions. Nor is it possible to determine the nature of ethical truths by purely empirical sources. This suggests that ethics are intuitive; that is, they are self-evident. The source of this evidence and what in fact we mean by being self-evident is open for considerable discussion. But generally it hinges on what Descartes suggested when he said "that which is, is clearly and distinctly true."[3]

The intuitionists hold that ethical properties are un-analyzable and indefinable, like the concept "blue." But at the same time, they assume ethical properties are known in the same manner we know what blue is. Ethical questions are not to be answered in terms of factual information or evidence but rather on whether they are true or false. This truth or falsity can be determined in the same way we can determine that a painting is ugly or beautiful. This judgment is not based on empirical experience nor on reasoning, but on recognition of the truth or falsity by means of self-evident knowledge. This knowledge is called intuition.[4]

Intuition is based on the interrelatedness of the whole through which we—as a part of the larger picture—can have knowledge about other parts. It is a form of uninferred or immediate knowledge that is reflected in our awareness of things like universals or duration. There is no immediate awareness—nor empirical evidence—of such things, but we are aware of them via our sense of "at-oneness" with the world in which we live. A very hard point of view to describe, it, nevertheless, is often associated with poets and mystics of all kinds. The common denominator in intuitive knowledge is that there is no rationale or sense of experience from which to trace the truth they feel they know.

There are some obvious problems with this approach. Not the least of these is the fact that people "intuit" totally different and confusing things.

Perhaps most confusing to the majority of persons, however, is the fact that such an intuitive justification is hard to understand as being different from motivation, cause, or even wishful thinking.

Noncognitive

The word cognitive is usually used to mean the reasoning process, those mental processes which we connect with understanding. Sometimes it is used to suggest utterances which are true by virtue of their intelligibility. When ethical theory uses the term *non-cognitive* it means truth by virtue of command or exclamation: expressions of arbitrary commitment or knowledge not connected with understanding. In this frame of reference, ethical judgments are not assertions of fact or statements describing actions at all. Rather they are something logically different and not open to either natural or non-natural justification. Three types of non-cognitive judgments will illustrate the point.

First is the denial of any ethical judgment. This accepts that what passes for ethical principles are simply expressions of arbitrary commitment. This view is often held by existentialists who suggest that a view like "honesty is good" refers to the fact that the person who is making the statement is committed to being honest but that this decision is arbitrary and without logic or justification.

The second position, like the first, asserts that ethical judgments are not provable and that they are little more than an effort to persuade others to your position. They are strong assertions not unlike stressing that "orange is the best color." Such a statement does not reveal any truth, nor can it be justified by either a source or an experience which supports it. At best such statements are explanations of what is desired by one and what others are pressured to accept.

The third, not unlike the first two, identifies ethical statements as evaluations. They are Kantian, meaning they are what the person would accept as a universal. When persons say, "Honesty is the best policy" what they are saying is, "I would accept honesty as a universal law for all to obey." If we say treating others with respect is good, we are stating that we have no objections if treating persons with respect becomes a universal law. It is not necessarily the speakers' own personal preferences, for in fact they might not want to be honest or to treat persons with respect, but they are willing to see these statements accepted as laws because of the advantages.

In many ways the modern idea of social law (even some forms of criminal law) falls into this category. We see behavior that is not acceptable in a personal way, but we are willing to see it made into a law. That was the case with the 55-mile-an-hour speed limit; it was such a law but now public opinion is changing it. It is not justified or even liked in many respects; it is only accepted.

Relativism

The assumption of ultimate agreement, of course,

is just an assumption. It is based on the fact that when human beings seek truth they tend to move toward ultimates which they believe are true for all persons. We have discussed some of these. The more we know about persons, however, the more we discover life to the Romans is not the same as life to persons in the West Indies. All persons do not use the same words, and the things they wish to describe are different. They appear to have little in common—at least in an ultimate sense—and there appears little they are willing to condemn as evil or unethical. Incest is seen as one of the few exceptions. But even the view of incest as evil is not as universal as we may imagine. Thus while relativism is not a new thesis, it has gained considerable popularity in the past few years because so many statements of universality have been challenged.

I can remember cowering under the covers of my bed when, as a child, my older brothers would read to me from *The Best Short Stories of 1936*. The theme of *1936* seemed to be that there were no unsolved murders; in the end the murderer is always caught. That idea somehow sustained me during those long evenings when I was trying to be brave. Since then I have learned that is not necessarily true. Nor is it true, as I then believed, that all people disliked murder, or would come to the aid of a child, or that money was the root of all evil. When I question myself about those beliefs, I realize that some of the reason for the difference is that I am older and am now just understanding the truths. I am also aware, however, that in some cases the reason I see these "truths" differently is that I have changed worlds. There are places where murder is not frowned upon, where money is still considered the root of all evil, and where children are taken care of.

Relativism states that different persons, different cultures, and different locations provide basic differences in the development of judgments. This includes moral judgments. This difference appears to be a matter of fact, and I am not inclined to challenge the social sciences and to question their identification of characteristics on this point.

Relativism also states that if this is true, such persons, societies, and cultures have different behavior and different ethical principles. They hold that these are intrinsically good for that person, or society, or culture. This may or may not be a matter of fact but seems to follow if (and only if) one holds that ethical principles and moral actions arise from the culture.

The third assertion of relativism is that if these things are true, a person cannot solve the conflicts that seem to appear within these judgments. No amount of rational thought, epistemological inquiry, or ultimate understanding, will end the conflict of these positions and provide some single acceptable position. Thus, if they are valid in their inception and cannot be resolved, it must follow, according to the relativists, that the existence of two or more conflicting opinions must be both possible and valid. In other words, there can be *several ethical ultimates at the same time.* The difference is a result of the differences in persons, societies, locations, and cultures.

There are two or three things of note to remember here. One is that we are not really sure we have the anthropological information necessary to make an ultimate statement about the likeness or the differences in and between human beings. The second is that it does not necessarily follow that because we cannot resolve ethical differences, the differences must be valid. And third, if there is no common universal among persons, then the universal nature of relativism is suspect. Consider, if every society held a validly different view of ethics, then all views—even relativism—would be valid only for the select societies that held them.[5]

The Good

In our discussion of ethics the word "good" will continue to come up as a definition. Over the years my father used to refer to an act or a fact as "being *so.*" It meant for him that the fact was beyond question and to a large extent was beyond discussion. For many, when we say we "want to be good" we refer to a condition that for us is "so." It suggests we have an understanding of what good means even if we cannot describe it.

However, many things are identified as good that have no moral value. When you say you're feeling good, you do not mean the same thing as when you say you have a good car. You know the difference without comment. However, when persons decide that money is good, meaning that money can be instrumental in achieving good, they often confuse the instrument with the goal.

In the study of ethics, a distinction is made, then, between moral and nonmoral good which will help us in our discussions. A moral value usually refers to persons, groups, traits, dispositions, emotions, motives, intentions, absolutes, or those things arising from persons or personality.

Things considered nonmoral are objects much like

97

cars, money, pain, or pleasure. At first it appears that many of these are moral because they deal with those things we considered good or bad. But, the point needs to be made that these later ones are basically things which are instrumental in bringing good.

Because the ethical task is to *do* good, our immediate job is to determine the criteria by which we identify intrinsic good, and eventually to identify those positions, views, persons who are instrumental in achieving that goodness. We are interested in trying "to be good," to establish "the good," to find "the good." Perhaps the place to start our search is with some understanding of the varied uses for the terms.

This is a good car...
This is a good sandwich...
It is good to see you...
Truth is good...
They are good players...
Spinach is good for you...
I was good...

These are all statements of value judgments, but they are not all the ultimate goals sought by ethical persons. Many are nonmoral judgments. The difference is somewhat complicated but important to our understanding. When one says "X is good" that means that anything like X or anything that has the primary characteristics of X is also good and that it is good in about the same manner and degree.

When pushed about why a sandwich is good, one is required to provide some more information. This information, in turn, is a more general value statement about what it means to be good. Thus, in our search, it is the larger value that we seek to identify, not the smaller, more limited one.

The sandwich is good because it excites my taste buds. This means the value of the sandwich is that it excites my taste buds. The sandwich then becomes a *means* to accomplish good and is not the good thing in itself. The good thing is the excited taste buds.

When we say that "it is a good car" we mean it is useful and will accomplish the purpose of a car whatever that means to us. We are not talking about its inherent value. When we say "it is good to see you" we mean that the experience is rewarding; perhaps physically as in you are beautiful, or psychologically as in terms of relief or peace. However, when we say "truth is good" we are suggesting that it is good in and of itself—inherently good—and we are not so much describing it as we are commending it.

When we remark that they "are good players" we mean that they play the game better than others, or accomplish what it is they set out to accomplish. It does not mean that they are better than the average person in terms of morality. When we say that "spinach is good for you" we generally mean spinach will make you healthy and strong. Spinach is not in and of itself good, but it leads to a good cause. Health may well be a moral judgment suggesting that it is good to be healthy in and of itself.

In the search for ethics we are primarily interested in the difference between things intrinsically good (things desirable in and of themselves) and instrumentally good (things good because they serve to bring about intrinsic goodness). Take some examples:

• Health is considered an intrinsic good. However,

it is also instrumental because health is often the means by which we bring happiness to others.
- Surgery is an example of fairly pure instrumentalism because it has little value in and of itself but is very valuable in bringing about the ultimate good.
- Money is a useful example of an instrumental good which over the years has become more and more an intrinsic good.
- Duty is an example of instrumental good which may legitimately be considered intrinsic as well.[6]

A list of what we consider to be intrinsically good might well include many things, most of which would be different. I would include a list like this:

friendship	warmth
beauty	awe
silence	mystery
ideas	love

A good friend who I consider very ethical, as well as deeply religious, has suggested a list like this:

travel	friendship
running	mystery
music	isolation
worship	organization (order)

The ethicists ask if we could suggest the common characteristics which we could look for in terms of identification of the "common good." It would be difficult for the two of us—my friend and I—but think of just how difficult for the whole community.

Common Characteristics
Over the centuries classical philosophers have

spent a great deal of effort desperately seeking a common characteristic to whatever humans considered to be good. The hope is that once that common ingredient is found it would serve as the basis for an ethical system. Such knowledge would help persons find a common ground to bring about an end to conflicts over values. Unfortunately, these philosophers have not been very successful. However, some basic suggestions have emerged and have been presented as the common ingredient: utility, happiness, pain, or pleasure. Upon some of these, philosophical systems (and, in some cases, religions) have been built.

More contemporary philosophers—certainly those in the nineteenth and twentieth centuries—have been a little more willing to suggest that no common characteristic exists for good. Or, if such a characteristic did exist, it would be so vague as to be of no value at all. For example, happiness means so many different things to so many different people that to suggest happiness as a common characteristic of good is basically meaningless.

One of the later philosophers to write about the idea of a chosen or common characteristics of good was the Englishman G. E. Moore. Moore's views are not without critics, and I am not suggesting him to you on the grounds that I think he is necessarily right. However, he does make some progress that will help us in our thinking. First of all, he recognized that things have both natural and non-natural characteristics. The color of an orange, for example, is a property that is based on sensory experience. We see the orange and it is orange. That property or characteristic is based on what we call a concrete fact.

Secondly, however, the oranges have characteristics that can only be known by introspection—that is, by my ability to look beyond what I see or hear or feel or taste or smell. I can say about the orange that it is beautiful or that it is good or that it is symbolic.

Moore is suggesting to us, then, that the property of good is a non-natural property. He reasons this way: If it were natural it would be concrete like orange. That when one says X is good, the X involved would be concrete, physical, and determined by the senses if the X were natural. Because it is not—that is, we do not have a physical sense of what is the common characteristic—then it must be non-natural. Being non-natural it represents a characteristic known by introspection, by intuition, from the individual.[7]

There were many classical as well as contemporary views of what this non-natural character of good might be. The most interesting appear to be Eudaemonism (happiness), Hedonism (pleasure), and Utilitarianism (utility) all of which are discussed in some detail in chapter 6.

Do we accept the most traditional views of human nature; in the final analysis, do most humans have the same desires, aspirations, and goals? If so, then there is not much problem identifying the nature of the good. In the past generation or so it has been assumed persons have their own aspirations and thus are not very much alike. If you accept this you have difficulty with a common good. In many ways our historical and social aspirations have been lost and the replacements have taken on cultural and educational temperament. At this point a common good becomes hard to find and difficult to understand.

In the 1930s the film of Margaret Mitchell's *Gone with the Wind* almost had to be reshot. The Hayes Office—the early conscience of the film industry—refused to allow distribution of a film which ended with what has now become the classic irony of the film: "Frankly, Scarlett, I don't give a damn." Today many films carry language that would seem crude in a Hong Kong brothel. Has good changed? Or has our view of the good changed? It makes a considerable difference.

The distinction between the desired and the desirable is still important. The concept of good is no less significant just because we have difficulty with the idea of a universal, or a higher good. It is probably true that if men and women were able to achieve their desires without conflict—and if those desires within them never clashed—then it would be unnecessary for intellectual or rational distinction to be made in moral life. Unfortunately, persons still live within these areas of conflict. Thus they will continue to struggle for means by which to select one sense of right over another.

CASE IN POINT. . .ORGAN TRANSPLANTS

The Department of Health and Human Services says: "HCFA should undertake efforts to help ensure that cadaver kidneys are not offered to foreign nationals unless it can be determined that no suitable U.S. recipient can be found." The important government study that may well affect your life goes on to say: "The call for an international, humanistic approach presents an attractive and important ideal. However, like any ideal, it must be examined in terms of associated realities and practical effects. In the present environment, where the U.S. demand for cadaver kidneys exceeds the supply, the application of this ideal involves some realities and effects that clearly undermine its value."

It goes on to list seven reasons why the "humanistic approach" is unrealistic: foreign nationals are more quickly serviced primarily because they take transplants better; therefore, U.S. residents wait longer; it would discourage national organ sharing (local areas would use their kidneys rather than making them available to another bank); medicare costs are increased; organ donation is jeopardized; post-transplant care is compromised; and valuable outcome data is lost (that is, we do not have statistics about how well these folks enjoyed their kidneys).

Questions for Consideration

- If the idea behind health care is that "everyone should be cared for" how can we establish requirements—other than health—for care?
- Why is being American any excuse to receive a needed transplant over being Korean?
- At what point does "practical" value overcome "humanitarian or Christian" value?

Quiz

Match by placing the letter of the term in column B in the space provided in column A.

A	**B**
1. ____ Reality is the particular and classifications are just names.	A. intuitionism
2. ____ Trying to justify values by empirical tests	B. noncognitive

3. ____ Ethics has both natural and non-natural characteristics.

C. nominalism

4. ____ Reality consists of universals, and particulars are only shadows.

D. G. E. Moore

5. ____ Denial of any ethical judgment acknowledges only arbitrary commitment.

E. instrumental

6. ____ Good in and of itself

F. empirical fallacy

7. ____ Non-naturalistic

G. meta-ethics

8. ____ The study of ethical principles or universals

H. intrinsic

9. ____ Good because it brings or promotes good

I. empirical

10. ____ Collecting data and evaluating it by way of the senses

J. realism

End Notes

1. Alan Tyree, "Divine Calling in Human History," 1984, W. Wallace Smith Lecture, Park College.
2. William K. Frankena, *Ethics* (New Jersey: Prentice-Hall, Inc., 1973), 98–99.
3. As quoted in Frankena, *Ethics*, 102.
4. Frankena, *Ethics*, 102–103.
5. Richard B. Brandt, "Disagreement and Relativism in Ethics" as quoted in William K. Frankena and John T. Granrose, *Introductory Readings in Ethics* (New Jersey: Prentice-Hall, Inc., 1974), 423–429.
6. The organization of this material is reflective of inquiries established by Frankena in *Ethics*, pp. 81–83 and Banner in *Ethics* pp. 13–14, 152–153.
7. G. E. Moore, *Principia Ethica* (Cambridge: Cambridge University Press, 1954), 59–91.

CHAPTER 6

THEORIES: IMPERATIVE, UTILITARIAN, EUDAEMONISM, AND HEDONISM

I believe in you so I guess I believe in what you believe.
—Sampson in *New Testament Follies*

When people are faced with the essential questions of life they want answers. "What shall I do?" What we want to know is what to do now, at this time, under these circumstances, and without a lot of soul-searching and/or hesitation. Under such conditions persons tend to be supportive of ethical systems. They understand the value of one set of principles that seem demonstrably superior over another. In the posturing of such systems, as well as in the criticism of them, questions of evaluation and application are all very important. But in the main the appeal is to the systematic nature of the presentation. There is a large variety of classical systems available and the contemporary world has produced a few of its own. The basic ethical considerations, however, might be seen in a more detailed examination of six of these: the moral imperative of Kant, eudaemonism, utilitarianism, hedonism, situational ethics, and existentialism in both Christian and atheistic varieties. Chapters on Christian ethics and the RLDS ethical theory will follow.

106

The Moral Imperative

One of the most basic ethical appeals was defined by Immanuel Kant in his work *Foundations of the Metaphysics of Morals.* Kant's ideas are not so much ethical principles as they are a means by which one can judge—or test—ethical principles. Kant's view is one of the two major displays of moral objectivity (the other being utilitarianism) and is a rational response to the social necessities of the community. It is an ethic of commitment which free men and women make to one another to form communities and seeks to test if a particular behavior is in keeping with the binding nature of this commitment.

Primary to Kant's philosophical inquiry is his concern about the ability to have real knowledge. He feels one cannot have such knowledge about God, freedom, or immortality; but certainly these are things about which one can think. And, in the thinking, one accepts that persons must have freedom or their actions are not a matter of choice. As we have seen earlier, where there is no choice there is no responsibility. It is only when persons are free to choose what they will do that they can seriously ask the question, "What shall I do?"

In his work Kant makes a distinction between what he calls the hypothetical imperative and the cognitive imperative. The hypothetical is binding to persons only to the extent that the ends to which the action is related are desired by the agent. Persons must go outside of themselves seeking to know the relationship between the action and the ends. The nature of our behavior is determined by the end designed for the action, so that the choice, if one exists, rests in determining the end not the action.

For many persons happiness is considered to be the primary end of behavior. So let us use happiness to illustrate. The hypothetical imperative might well dictate that knowing happiness is the goal we are trying to accomplish. Thus to *know* what would produce the happiness desired would ethically obligate persons to behave in that fashion. This could seem to be a valid understanding of behavior. However, it is illustrative only of the hypothetical imperative.

Kant does not accept happiness as either the goal or the end of human moral behavior. Morality is a demand—a command from the cosmos—which must be maintained in its own right and is not an end or a means to intermediate ends. And most assuredly it is not the promotion of happiness. Suppose you hold the position, ''I will not steal because if caught I will go to jail and that would not make me happy.'' While the end of happiness may continue to be persistent, the acceptance of the means is contingent—almost arbitrary. Suppose I decide that going to jail would make me happy. I would then be deciding that it was acceptable to steal because stealing is not the question; happiness is. Kant suggests that one cannot be counted on to act in a given way or to accept behavior of any kind as long as the means is unrelated to the end in terms of morality. If the goal of morality is to be happy, anything that makes me happy is acceptable moral behavior. And, Kant assures us, that is not the case.

Morality is restricted to objective reality. Kant will accept as morally good only those things which are determined by reason and, therefore, are not subjective or held as the goal by virtue of being valid for every rational being. Moral good is then
108

that which is its own means and end. This is what he calls the "categorical imperative." To act as a moral being is to act under the obligation of the categorical imperative, which is binding upon the will and, therefore, law. The hypothetical imperative is not really an imperative because the end is subject to change and that makes the imperative contingent. A contingent imperative is irrational.

The categorical imperative is just that, an imperative. It is the consistent, noncontradictory requirement which, Kant would say, "holds good for everyone having reason and will."[1] A moral individual cannot propose a law of behavior that is not equally as valid for each and every other human individual; that is the rule if reason applies to all persons. Obviously reason is equally true in every case and allows no exceptions for an individual's favor. In each and every case in which I seek action that is of my own interest, I do so at the cost of reason.

Kant uses the examples of suicide and false promises to pay a debt. He suggests that while they may seem to be of advantage to the individual, they are irrational. The irrationality is seen in the categorical imperative. The single maxim of the imperative is: "Act only according to that maxim by which you can at the same time will that it should become universal law."[2]

That quaint language holds a very simple position. If you want to consider an action—like suicide—then you must test this against the universal law that "all persons must commit suicide." Not, you see, that they *may*, but that they *must*. Because it becomes obvious that such a law would be totally irrational when gauged against the thinking of the rational community, it must be assumed that the

109

action for the individual is wrong. The same would be true in paying a debt. Do you think it would be rational for everyone in the community to make debts with the full knowledge that the law requires nonpayment? Such a community could not function; it would be totally irrational. Thus when you consider this action on your part, while it may sound good to you at the moment, it cannot be considered ethical.

This is not a utilitarian position. The difference may seem small, but it is important. For Kant the purpose of not stealing pens at the post office is not because of the final effect of the act—that there will be no pens at the post office—but that to universalize the stealing of pens at the post office would be self-defeating to anyone who would use the post office. The problem lies in the positive side of the issue. Kant's ethic lies in our willingness to see our wishes universalized and made a duty. Early in life I learned to put cream in my iced tea. A habit, I hear, that is not now being universally adopted. I can imagine a law which would say "put cream in your iced tea" and accept it as a universal law. It would not bother me; it would not seem to be oppressive and would, in the long run, cut down explanation time considerably. The issue, however, is not "should everyone drink cream with ice tea" but rather "should each one's tastes be made into my laws."

The first is not a rule for ethical behavior. The second is a rule. If persons are to be controlled only by self-interests, they will find their actions determined by forces morally blind and unacceptable to the community. However, if such individual decisions are made on the basis of the needs of the

110

rational community and their own membership in that community, then one can determine behavior in a large measure from the community. It is not an ethic founded on the actions of the community, but an ethic that emerges from realizing that the community has a practical response to the categorical imperative. After all, the point of ethics is to be obedient to the imperative—the command—and is not concerned with advantages to be gained by obedience.

What if my question was this: "Shall I marry Annie Laurey with the golden hair?" Certainly the point in this decision is not that everyone in the world should marry Annie. I may think that all would want to or that she is worthy. But do I really think such a law is the means for making my decision? Of course not, Kant would say, you are confusing the obligatory with the permissible. Obligation, as he defines it, is the necessity of free persons to act under the categorical imperative, thus to be involved in actions that are either commanded or forbidden. Yet there is a vast amount of other decisions that must be made. These decisions will be based on what he calls the permissible. The permissible being those neutral things for which there are neither command nor prohibition, only the questions of nonmoral concern. Moral duties are a matter of obligation.

Happiness

Before discussing happiness as the source of ethical behavior (eudaemonism), it will be helpful to make two distinctions. The first has to do with the meaning of happiness. We probably will not agree on exactly what it means, but it is important to define the parameters of what is included in happiness as an ethical theory. The second will be to make a distinction between pleasure and happiness, for in this study they are different things.

While there are many things that happiness might well be, there are three classifications that help in its identification: First of all, there are those things which produce joy or excitement (the opposite of gloom or sadness) and thus are pleasant. A second would be those things which are the fulfillment of what we want—getting our own way. The opposite of this would be frustration or anger, even perversity. Happiness is concerned with getting our way, not with what we want or what in the long run will be best for us.

The third is the definition that we will be using here. Happiness also means satisfaction, a sense of peace or tranquility, or a feeling of well-being that extends beyond any given event or response. It is that sense of acceptance not only with others but with oneself which carries on and becomes a way a direction for life. If this is the case, then to suggest that the ethical principle would be to act in a way to bring happiness or avoid unhappiness would be valid only if seen as long-term, progressive satisfaction with one's self and with life.

The second distinction we need to make is between happiness and pleasure. The distinction is somewhat arbitrary, I believe, but is important to make to understand the idea of happiness as an ethical goal. As we have suggested, happiness represents one's satisfaction with existence as a whole. This kind of happiness cannot be identified with pleasure for, as we are all aware, it is possible to endure a considerable amount of pain, hardship, bodily and mental destructions and still remain on the whole happy. While it is certainly obvious that a happy life will include some pleasure, the reverse is not true. All happiness is pleasurable though not all pleasure is happy.

We can push this definition and distinction too far. It would be hard to defend the position that bad people are basically unhappy. But all events being equal, we might agree that one's total goodness tends to make him or her happy. The important point for us here is that happiness is not *the good* but is rather instrumental in bringing about a good. A person seeks the ethical principle—do that which will bring one the greatest happiness—in order to arrive at an ideal state. The state we seek seems to be well-being or the goal of life or fulfillment. We then say that it is *good* to be happy, not that happiness is goodness. The end we seek through the instrument of happiness is well-being.[3]

Happiness and goodness have a great deal in common. Among other things they represent a state of being in which we have a great interest but which we have never really identified. We can generally picture a state of happiness or the idea of goodness. But we acknowledge both of them most often in their absence. Things are not as happy as we would like them. We are not experiencing what we envision. Therefore, we carry with us this idealized version without having any realistic experience with it. Most of us are happy a good deal of the time. Lacking happiness, we are at least not unhappy. But perfect happiness, like well-being and perfection, seems to exist for us in the desired rather than in the attained.

Happiness as ethical principle, then, is different

from hedonism or the search for pleasure or even a collection of events which make us happy. It is an ethical principle which states that given a choice, one must make the decision about behavior with long-term, total-person, wholistic, and community relationships in mind. Such decisions are mindful that what we seek as a goal is not immediate pleasure or temporary gratification but a sense of happiness.

It is within this context that ethical persons consider why people often act against their best interests. That is, they act altruistically. If the goal is happiness, then the effect of behavior is often the key. John S. Mill has suggested it is better to be "a human being dissatisfied than a pig satisfied." In the definition of our lives, we are often aware that we would "rather be right than president," would rather be comfortable than dressed in worldly finest, or would rather struggle to climb the mountain than to leave the mountain unclimbed. Happiness is not pleasure nor is it necessarily joy. But rather, happiness is satisfaction: the internal feelings of integrity and the peace that comes from doing what you think is right rather than what is easy. Sometimes it is also true that happiness is the willingness to give what you have—even your life—for another. Are such persons seeking pleasure or even utility? Probably not. More likely they see the good as that which calls them to actions which, though momentarily destructive, are destined for their ultimate happiness.

Utilitarianism

Like Kant's categorical imperative, utilitarianism is a modern world reaction to the challenge of traditional ideas. In an assumption born of the Enlightenment, morality was challenged to be consistent with the understanding available from empirical evidence. In the final analysis, morality was required to have some independence of thought from its theological base. Kant's suggestions contain a rational morality. In utilitarianism we discover an ethical claim based on both personal and public understandings of pleasure and pain and their relation to happiness. This teaching was articulated by numerous philosophers but is best explained through the teachings of Jeremy Bentham and John S. Mill.

While Bentham belonged to the age of the Enlightenment, he rejected any concept of the natural rights of persons. Rather he felt actions and purpose emerged rationally from a person's experience. Investigations into personal experience and moral behavior revealed that empirical awareness establishes happiness as the end (purpose) of human activity. Behavior is accepted or rejected on the basis that it promotes or discourages happiness. First Bentham and later Mill termed this "utility." What they meant is that utility is the basic principle on which the acceptance of any public policy can be measured. The justification behind a law lies in the good or pleasure which would come from the action and from the absence of pain or distress prevented by such a law.[4]

Realizing that for Bentham the search for ethical behavior is at the same time a search for law, we can understand why he imposes a sort of moral calculus. He determined that legislation must be directed toward achieving the greatest amount of happiness for the largest number of persons. In this quantitative ethic each person counts as one and

115

only one. The whole concept of ethics is found in directing a person's actions to the production of the largest amount of this happiness.

Like the true hedonists, these utilitarians know the value of pain and pleasure. And in the calculations, pain and pleasure are experiences that stand in dimension. Even if persons may be seen equally, the intensity, duration, certainty, remoteness, purity, and extent are all a part of the mathematical account to be taken. It is not just pleasure but pleasure calculated.

Over the years there have been some serious questions about the role of pleasure and happiness. It is true, for example, that there are persons for whom pain produces pleasure, or who get great pleasure in doing something they do not like to do because of their love for another. Bentham makes a simple case. First of all, persons are never motivated by pleasure to act against their self-interest. He rejects as a philosophical fallacy the idea that individuals seek any other end than pleasure and the avoidance of pain. If your definitions of pleasure and/or pain are different than the rest of the world that is of little note; it does not change his thesis.

Certainly in utilitarianism, the happiness of the individual is sometimes restricted, but only in the immediate sense, not in the long range. Private ethics that rest on a rule of prudence (that is, duty to oneself) cannot violate the rule of beneficence (duty to a neighbor). Right action in terms of ethical behavior is any action which secures the greatest happiness (in intensity) for the greatest number (the largest count of individuals) for the greatest amount of time. At the root of persons' actions under such a rule are the social feelings of humankind by which we identify our desire to live in unity with the other members of our community.

Hedonism

The ethical principle identified as hedonism is based on the association of good with pleasure and evil with pain. For the hedonist the right course of action is that action which produces at least as much pleasure as it does pain. The more hedonistic the ethicist is, the more pleasure is demanded in this balance. For the hedonist the formula is simple: happiness equals pleasure and pleasure equals happiness. The goal of human activity is to achieve pleasure. Pleasure is intrinsically good—that is, good within itself—and thus, pleasure is the goal, the end of action. Pleasure is not an instrument to get you to what is important, it *is* what is important. In a larger sense, we must suppose, such a point of view could allow for the fact that under some conditions pain can be pleasure (for example, when one thinks she has lost a leg and discovers through pain that she has not). But hedonism has historically been free from such ideas.

Pleasure then is both the means and the end. Pleasantness is the criteria that is used to determine intrinsic goodness in those things which are seen as ends, as well as those that are seen as means to those ends. Jeremy Bentham, primarily a utilitarian, has suggested what he calls the seven tests of hedonism—a sort of pleasure calculus reflective of utility's tests that can be applied to any proposed action or event to see if the anticipated pleasure is high enough and the pain low enough. The amount of pleasure should be measured against its intensity, duration, certainty, propinquity, fecundity, purity, and extent.[5]

Intense, long, certain, speedy, fruitful, pure
such marks in *pleasure* and in *pain* endure,
Such pleasures seek if private be thy end
If it be *public,* wide let them *extend*
Such pain avoid, whatever be thy view;
If pains must come, let them extend to few.[6]

Years ago when I first started teaching at Graceland College, I lived in Lamoni, Iowa. The closest restaurant of any possible excitement at the time was fifty-five miles away at a somewhat larger, small Iowa town. The buffet-style meal was marvelous. They had a variety of meats and cheeses, salads and desserts, plus things like shrimp and Waldorf salad. So, with opportunities limited, it was entertainment for some to make that long drive, eat until they could hardly stand, and then make the long trip back. But if any of us were hedonists—and I must assume that we were not— we would have approached this trip differently. Using Bentham's list we might well go through this exercise.

In deciding to make the trip one must consider just how great the pleasure of eating will be (intensity); how long that pleasure will last (duration); how certain we are that the restaurant will be open and that the food will be as good as we remembered (certainty); just how near to us it is, and to what degree will the fact that we have to drive a long distance diminish the pleasure (propinquity); will the event itself produce pleasure, that is, will the eating of the food provide an added sense of well-being (fecundity); will the event be pure, that is, will it be all pleasure or be-
118

fore long will the pain of being full make one question the wisdom of eating all that was consumed (purity); and last but not least, what was the expense of the pleasure; did it bring pleasure only to me or to the one driving or the one on a diet (extent).

Given that persons know what they want, what gives them pleasure, and to what degree their individual pleasure is more valid than that of the community, hedonism seems very straightforward. It would be hard to deny that many of us make decisions on the basis of pain and pleasure. It is hard to argue against. We do things because we want to, because they feel good, or because we enjoy them. Most of us make this decision about our entertainment, to lesser degrees about our friends, our jobs, or the sort of car we drive. True, for most persons there are other choices and limitations: we are limited by money, opportunity, expectation, perhaps even other ethical goals. But, if we are honest, we will acknowledge that pleasure is a significant goal in our lives.

The systems available to us within hedonism, then, are systems which acknowledge a pleasure sort of response. When we must make a choice about behavior or actions we will choose the one that will produce the most pleasure (with duration, intensity, etc.) and the least amount of pain. We can and will interpret that in many ways, but basically that is the key. Hedonism is frowned upon by Christians and altruistic persons as being selfish. That may well be the problem. Being selfish is considered unethical because of ethical assumptions we make about responsibilities and obligations to the community. Is a selfish hedonist possible?

In a brief summary we can see four important, and very different theories about ethics. These are all assumptions about the nature of ethics, and each reflects a view which has had literally millions of followers. Kant seeks a moral objective discovered by the rational mind. He uses as his "test" our willingness to allow our *wishes* to become *laws,* and seeks an ethical principle which supports only that behavior by which we could universally live.

The other three theories are associated with views of happiness as the goal of life. Eudaemonism bases ethical decision on the promise such action will produce happiness—meaning *well-being* and long-term personal satisfaction. Utilitarianism seeks a happiness which is interpreted as the greatest amount of good for the largest number of a given (select) community. Hedonism, on the other hand, interprets happiness in terms of pleasure and builds its somewhat complicated system on levels and degrees of pleasure.

Quiz

Answer the following by marking the questions true or false.

_____ 1. Kant's moral imperative is the only ethic based on moral objectivity.

_____ 2. A hypothetical imperative represents the desires of the person involved.

_____ 3. The categorical imperative is binding upon the will and is therefore law.

_____ 4. Kant's view is utilitarian.

_____ 5. Happiness and pleasure are not the same for utilitarians.

_____ 6. Bentham rejects any idea of natural rights.

_____ 7. According to Bentham, persons never act against their self-interest.

_____ 8. Hedonism is a kind of moral calculus.

_____ 9. Fecundity means no pain.

_____10. Hedonism considers selfishness to be unethical.

End Notes

1. Immanuel Kant, *Critique of Practical Reason,* translated by Lewis W. Beck (Chicago: University of Chicago Press, 1949), 131–132.
2. _____ *Fundamental Principles of the Metaphysic of Morals,* translated by Lewis W. Beck (Chicago: University of Chicago Press, 1949), 80.
3. Hastings Rashdall, "Happiness, Pleasure, and the Good" as quoted in William K. Frankena and John Granrose, *Introductory Readings in Ethics* (New Jersey: Prentice–Hall, Inc., 1974), 345–346.
4. The idea of utility was established by Jeremy in *Introduction to the Principles of Morals and Legislation* (New York: Bobbs Merril, 1948).
5. Bentham as quoted in Frankena, *Readings,* 135.
6. Frankena, *Readings,* 135.

CASE IN POINT...ABORTION

The question of abortion is made even more difficult because it is both a moral and a legal question. At the moment abortion is legal in the United States. That, of course, does not make it ethical. An important point to remember is that for the majority it is not abortion that is wrong, it is murder which is wrong. Abortion is a medical process like having a tooth pulled or an abscessed tooth drained. Thus it is not abortion we are concerned with, it is the outcome.

Those who favor abortion or who, at least, are not against it, make their case based on the belief the fetus is not a person and thus abortion is not murder; they add some form of one of the following three arguments:

1. Abortion is a personal matter that involves one's own conscience, thus it is not a matter of social or public decision. Women have a right not to have their bodies used in a manner of which they do not approve. In any other case, they argue, both the society and the law would support this claim.

2. The fetus is an extension of the female tissue and thus the woman has the same rights over it as she does over other parts of the body. They would claim that abortion is no different than any other surgery.

3. And finally, abortions are therapeutic. That is, they are done to solve a problem—be it physical or psychological—and thus are to be seen as healing. They are needed for the prevention of physical or mental problems that will exist without them.

On the other side the arguments against abortions tend to be formed around one of the following three arguments:

1. Abortions cause death because persons (personality) begin at the moment of conception. Such a death is murder. Murder is both illegal and immoral and thus is unethical and should not be done.

2. Abortion is an act of self-centeredness. It results from choices based on the individual wants and wishes without any regard to the desires of the unborn, or the society in which the unborn may well make a contribution.

3. Because abortion, by definition, involves the life of more than one person (at least the mother and the child, and preferably even the father) then the question is a social issue.

A fourth argument is often introduced. It is not unlike the others but is important because the source is the basis of the truth. It says that God commands against murder. Even, they would point out, the secular humanists are willing to define murder as immoral and illegal. The abortionists' argument counters, as could be expected, that because abortion does not cause murder (there is no person until birth), then God could not have commanded against it.

In considering abortion look at the following questions:

1. Because murder is defined as illegally taking a life, and because abortion is legal, it could not be murder. Discuss.

2. If abortion were not legal, would it still be right? Or, if illegal but not morally wrong, should persons be involved in it?

3. If conception is the beginning of life, and thus cannot be violated, is there any point in which a child can be "terminated"? What about cases like rape or illness? If one person will die because of medical complications, how do the authorities decide which one?

4. Is it the matter of life that makes the difference? If so, why is it considered legitimate to execute prisoners, or to allow (encourage) heroes to die for their country? To what degree is the individual's (the baby's) choice a matter of importance?

CHAPTER 7

MORE THEORIES: SITUATIONAL ETHICS AND EXISTENTIALISM

Man is nothing other than his project, he exists only insofar as he realizes himself, thus he is nothing other than the whole of his actions, nothing other than his life.

—Jean-Paul Sartre

Joseph Fletcher made a name for himself some years ago when he suggested that we should let some 10 million people in India who were starving, go ahead and starve. He called this ethical behavior. The idea behind this suggestion was not inhumane but rather, given the situation in India, considered as the loving thing to do. Granted some 10 million were starving. Given the economic conditions there, and because of their attitude about birth control, it was estimated that in a decade there might well be an additional 10 million people and they also would be starving. Thus, if we allowed those now alive but starving to receive food and did nothing about their economic condition or their birth control, in effect we were condemning 20 million persons to starvation. Thus, as much as we dislike the situation, it would be more expressive of our love for them if we allowed them to die.

Both Fletcher's facts and options may be open to serious question. Most of us would insist that there must be another solution. Fletcher himself was not

124

suggesting he liked this or that he was not willing to work toward some other way out. He only contended that given the situation, he was selecting the most loving thing to be done.

Situation Ethics

The ethical theory identified with Fletcher grew as a criticism of systems based on exclusive rules of behavior. Fletcher was astonished by the limitations placed on behavior by rules which, as he saw it, did not provide the results that people intended from their behavior. In its initial stages situation ethics appeared to be a rush to the extremes. Perhaps even to the belief that there can be no absolutes and, thus, no general rules by which to live. But this is not really the case. This ethical position is based on the assumption that each and every situation is different and thus calls for different action. Ethical behavior brings love to the situation.

In situation ethics there is no intrinsic human nature. It acknowledges no behavior common to all persons. If there were such a human behavior then under like situations persons would act on the basis of that behavior. Not true say the defenders of situation ethics. What is right for one person is not necessarily right for every other person even under the same circumstances. Nor would it be right for the same person under different circumstances.

Let us go back for a moment to the ethical question asked at the beginning of the book. We have a student in ethics class who has cheated on her examination and been caught. She cheated primarily because she was afraid, knowing that if she did not pass the course she would not graduate and, in turn, would lose her job. She needed her job to take care of herself and her young family.

The ethical question arises when the instructor needs to take action. Should he fail the woman as threatened or allow her to pass so that her needs and the needs of her family can be met? There are a lot of things at stake here including the university's standards, the whole lesson of ethics, the state of the family and welfare of the children, and the instructor's integrity as well as his sense of humanitarianism. The rule is clear in this case: ''A person who cheats on an examination will fail.'' But the purpose of the rule is not that clear and the circumstances (the situations) are different and unique.

For situation ethics the behavior in this case is not as clear as the rule would suggest. There are larger concerns. Of concern is the seeming conflict of ethics, the fact that more than one rule applies and seems to be in opposition. There is the fact that a member of the human community comes into conflict with a member in the university community. Does the fact that problems which seem clear among professional students do not seem to be clear—in fact are in opposition—in the case in which one is unexpectedly thrust into the role of student? After all, the young woman did not take the course to learn ethics but to keep her job. The rules then may well be, and often are, incompatible. There is nothing absolute to do and because the rules are in conflict, there is nothing else to do but draw conclusions from each unique situation.

Most persons will make an effort at this point to bring into play a hierarchical view of ethical rules—a ladder of rules—based on a selection of rules rather than absolute responses. Nothing is required when the rules conflict other than that we seek to do the most important or most significant thing. We might well decide, for example, that the university's reputation is more valuable than the young woman's job. Situation ethicists would point out that all that is being done here is that we are picking the rule that we like the most. There is no reason for any one rule to be any more important than the other—if they were inherently more important they would not have appeared in conflict in the first place—thus the selection is arbitrary. We recognize that the more general a rule, the freer we are from an obligation to it. By the same token, the more specific the rule is, the more helpful it can be in a given situation. But the situationists seek freedom from all of these: from the obligation of strict rules, from the helplessness of general rules, and from the evaluation and arbitrary selection of conflicting rules.

They suggest instead a positive proclamation of moral spirit. Instead of rules they rely on a view of morality expressed and identified by the spirit. To act morally is to act within this spirit. Because the key to behavior is the spirit, it is dependent on the uniqueness of the moment rather than on some set of behavior patterns. The spirit is effectively an intuitive response based on experience, understanding, and love. It is primarily a wholistic response to the human situation.

This injection of ethical intuition provides the basis of a response which allows us to address specific situations. This moral intuition is not a fleeting concept grasped momentarily by the alert mind. It is not a truth hovering about the absolute, waiting for some receptive mind to pick it up. Rather, it results from serious and continued personal study and questioning concerning general beliefs, expectations, directions, and values. All of these are designed to help you understand where you stand morally and to understand that where you stand is constantly in a state of flux directed by the unique nature of a given situation.

If it is our contention that each and every person is different and the nature of that difference prescribes different relationships, then we are supporting what is sometimes called *ethical individualism* or, when considered more as a system, *ethical egoism*. Basically these are efforts to recognize the individual against the community ethic. Situation ethics is beyond this. Moral intuition is not persons deciding to do what they want or what is good for them, but rather what they understand to be good for the persons involved in this particular case. They may well have a goal, a direction, a need; that is not the question. The question is behavior in this situation.

Many things are involved in assessing the situation. One of these is the selection of evils. For most of us, most of the time, our choice about what to do is not a choice between right and wrong. It is often a choice between evils. We are called upon to make some decisions about which action will do the least harm rather than, as we would like, which is good and which is bad. The person who must choose between killing to save the family and allowing them to die does not have a correct moral choice—only select degrees of bad choices.

In addition, in assessing a situation, one must be aware of the concept of consent. For most readers, breaking into a house is high on the list of things not to do. But in a given situation you might well feel that it is acceptable. The level of acceptability is based on the fact that you know the person whose home it is, so you can assume an implied agreement. Under the circumstances they will "understand" and see your action as less a violation than others. Thus breaking into a home is a situation that would alter tremendously, based on implied consent *via* knowledge of the owners.

There is also the question of the greater demand. This is not a question of goodness but of necessity. Sometimes it becomes obvious that one demand is given higher priority because of necessity. Often this priority is seen as a limitation, maybe even something that cannot be counted in the question of ethics. Suppose you and I are both hanging by our fingertips from a rock ledge 300 feet in the air. It does not matter how we got there. You start to slip and ask me to help you. To add any weight to my fingers would mean that I will slip. The demand for me to hang on is made greater by the fact that I cannot help, even if I let go. All of my energy is taken up and to use less energy in my own behalf will not save you at my expense. We will both die if I try to help. I cannot win in such a situation; neither can you. But neither of us is acting unethically.

Unattainable time is another aspect to be considered in a given situation. You are an officer in a submarine during wartime. In closing the hatch during an emergency dive one of your men catches his thumb. To go up again will expose all to death; to go down you must close the hatch all the way. You order the man's thumb cut off. This gruesome but actual situation makes its point. There may well have been other solutions, all sorts of good and bad that could have been done differently. But the

129

situation here made this more an ethical imperative than a choice. Any sort of *ought* ("I ought not to disfigure this man") would have implied a *can* ("I can do something to save his thumb"). The situation, however, was such that time prevented anything but immediate action. In the situation the action becomes right because time was the determining factor. Such action might never again be right—but it was then.

What situation ethics is suggesting is that one must be in a position to deal with action not as if a rule applies to every situation, but accepting and rejecting the implications of such rules according to the situation. Thus they may accept a rule against harming a person and a rule against stealing. Yet in any given situation they may decide that harming a person and stealing are necessary. This is true because of the situation not the rules. Rules and absolutes then must be interpreted so that they do not become mechanical replies or legal solutions. The interpretation is one that applies the limitations—the intuitive spirit—in the widest manner.

So far we have dealt with the need to recognize the context from which we act—the situation of the action we must evaluate in order to act. Now we need to take a moment to look at the basic principle on which the decision to act is taken.

J. LeClercq reports that Jesus Christ "reacted particularly against code morality and against causity"[1] and that his attitude "toward code morality [was] purely and simply one of reaction."[2] Situation ethics responds to situations on the basis of love, the difference being that "love's decisions are made situationally, not prescriptively."[3] When love directs rather than laws or rules, the decisions of the conscience are relative. The situationist enters every decision-making encounter fully aware of the ethical maxims of the community and tradition. These are treated with respect and intelligent acknowledgment. However, the situationists are perfectly willing to sacrifice either in any situation where love is better served by doing so. Of all the commandments of ethics, only the commandment of love is categorically good. Only one thing is intrinsically good, namely love—nothing else at all.

Existentialism

Existentialism is primarily ethical in its concern. It addresses itself to a person's place in the cosmos and the behavioral implications of that place. It assumes there is some morally appropriate and inappropriate behavior, but in general it dispenses with any pretense of absolute *a priori* values.

Existentialism is a contemporary position based on a long line of absolute idealists and rationalists. First recognized in the writings of the Dane, Soren Kierkegaard, in the middle of the nineteenth century, it reflects a combination of the great joys and the potential horror of human freedom. Modeled by the late nineteenth-century German, Friedrich Nietzsche, and Martin Heidegger and Jean-Paul Sartre of the twentieth, it serves as a label for a widely described philosophy of human nature. While only Sartre of the above mentioned would appear happy with the label, it is, nevertheless, reflective of a vast movement that has deeply affected the modern generation.

Within this tradition are such widely held points of view as those of the Christian philosopher Gabriel Marcel, the Jewish existentialist Martin

Buber, as well as Simone de Beauvoir and Jean-Paul Sartre who speak for atheistic existentialism.[4]

What existentialists have in common is their agreement that existence precedes essence. Using Sartre as our spokesman we must assume this means that persons have existence first. Following that, persons will begin to form themselves, eventually being able to distinguish themselves from one another. Persons are what they conceive and determine themselves to be. There is no predetermined nature to them. Persons are nothing other than what they are or what they will become. The first principle being that "man is nothing other than what he makes himself."

This view assumes no creator. It assumes persons were not designed to be some person before their creation. Because persons are the cause of who they are, they are also responsible for what they are and that which they will be. They must assume total responsibility for their essence. A man or a woman springs up into the world and at that point must make decisions about what he or she will be, not necessarily what they wish, but what they will be.

In a more important sense when the existentialists say that persons determine themselves, they mean that they have made the choices which determine what they are. But it means more than this. It also means that they are responsible for others. Why? Because in the process of establishing values about who and what they plan to be, they are also establishing values about the nature of being. We choose against evil and, thus, define what evil is. We choose to be a certain person and in that value we help define what it means to be a person.

There are some key words in the ethical philosophy of existentialism which shed considerable light, not only on their position, but on the whole study of ethics. One of these is the term *anguish.* The total responsibility that follows when persons realize they have chosen not only for themselves but for all persons, produces a deep and profound uneasiness. In the performance of action, the existentialists must ask themselves "What if everyone did this?" In the answer lies the troubling thought. It is what Kierkegaard identified as the anguish of Abraham who must choose not only to obey God but, at the same time, to make assumptions about the validity of the angel and the understandings of the message. The leader who makes decisions knows the anguish even more clearly, for this is the person who understands that the value of the choice lies in the fact a choice is made.

A second significant term is *abandonment.* By this existentialists mean that God does not exist (at least not as we have imagined) and we must, therefore, deal with the consequences of God's absence. No existentialist finds hope in God's death. Rather they recognize that with God's disappearance (and it is more a disappearance than a death) one loses every possibility of an *a priori* (before experience) or absolute truth. Consequently persons recognize this abandonment when they realize that there is no force looking out for them, taking care of them, or accepting blame for the mess the world is in. We are, as they say, condemned to be free.

They use the word *condemned* because they feel that most of us do not like our freedom. Despite what we say we do everything in our power to give it away. Our freedom means that we can decide if we will accept or deny passion; it means we can give or deny meaning to our lives; it means we are free from determination by responsible forces outside ourselves. Likewise, we are free from motives or from legal answers to our questions. More important, however, we are free from antecedently fixed or established values. Human experience creates value; value is not discovered or uncovered. It is in our choosing that we define what a value is; and, at the same time, we recognize these values are absurd. In using the term *absurd* they mean the values are irrational, they are not based on reason or on the nature of things. They are valuable because we make them so. But it means as well that we are free from any values that exist prior to our experience.

Thus we ask, "Am I really the kind of person who has the right to act in such a way that humanity might guide itself by my action?"[6] We recognize as well that we are the one by whom truth comes into the world. Thus every person is responsible for carrying the weight of the world as the author of events made real and valuable by personal choices.

In our choices we discount evil and decide upon good. And in this process we determine what good is. Thus Sartre can say: "I am responsible for myself and for everyone, and I create a certain image of man which I choose; in choosing myself, I choose man."[7] Because individuals are absolutely free to choose their own world and their world's meaning, they are absolutely responsible for them. Insofar as persons have no predetermined nature, they cannot place the responsibility for what happens, or their choices, on anyone else. Thus it is that persons are condemned to be responsible.

We now have two more ethical theories. Both are

built on more immediate principles than those discussed in the earlier chapter. The first, situation ethics, assumes that the universal, if there is one, is love. It recognizes that acting in love, however, will never be possible if one operates from a rule or an absolute. Every situation is unique and calls for a unique reaction. It is in understanding the situation and acting in love out of the true understanding that ethics emerge. The existentialists on the other hand base their ethics on responsibility. Assuming that each person is primarily responsible for his or her own actions—and thus for creating individual personhood—ethics emerge from those actions which assume such responsibility.

CASE IN POINT. . . CONSCIENCE

Joanmarie Smith, in her book *Morality Made Simple But Not Easy,* lists three functions of the conscience. They are:

1. To make us aware that we are responsible for our actions and that we should do good in this world. It serves to remind us of this fact. To act without conscience is to act as if there were no obligations to do good.

2. A conscience tells us what is the right choice in a particular situation, assuming of course that we already have a "formed or complete" conscience. The idea is that persons have a sense of right or wrong which they are born with—or which develops very early in their childhood training—and this sense can be brought to bear at a given point when a decision must be made. Such a sense of conscience is expressed in a mood, or feeling, or even an internal pressure.

3. It serves then not only to tell us what is right,

but it pressures us to do that which is right. We will feel imbalances, or out-of-sorts, or ashamed until we do right.[5]

There is considerable question about conscience. Some persons seem to have a sense of right and wrong but it is different from our own. Others have no such sense at all. Consider the following questions:

1. If we all had a conscience and it was available prior to—or at least at—birth, then would we not all have the same sense of right and wrong?

2. Why do we seek ethical principles if we have a conscience? Are there any principles that seem to be held ''in conscience'' that are the same?

3. Consider if hope is the same as conscience. Look at this statement about hope by Tennyson.

> Behold, we know not anything;
> I can but trust that good shall fall
> at last—far off—at last, to all
> And every winter change to spring.

Quiz

Answer the following by providing a short answer in the space provided.

1. The key to situation ethics is _____.

2. What is meant by a hierarchy of ethical rules?

3. Describe what is meant by the philosophical term *ethical egoism?*

4. Give three examples of *a priori* ethical values.

   a.

   b.

   c.

5. Existentialism seems to contradict the traditional Christian story of creation. Think about how existentialism is supportive of the traditional story and give two examples.

   a.

   b.

6. What do the existentialists mean by the term absurd?

End Notes

1. Jacques LeClercq, *Christ and the Modern Conscience,* 59–61 as quoted in Joseph Fletcher, *Situation Ethics* (Philadelphia: The Westminster Press, 1960), 130.
2. As quoted in Joseph Fletcher, *Situation Ethics* (Philadelphia: The Westminster Press, 1960), 139.
3. Fletcher, 145.
4. Philip Mariet (ed.), *Jean Paul Sartre: Existentialism and Humanism* (London: Negel and Methuen and Company, 1948) for general information.
5. Joanmarie Smith, *Morality Made Simple But Not Easy* (Allen, Texas: Argus Communication, 1986), 71–75.
6. Fletcher, 21.
7. Julius Weinberg and Keith Yandell, *Ethics* (New York: Holt, Rinehart, and Winston, Inc., 1971), 9.

CHAPTER 8

SPECIAL RULES FOR SPECIAL PEOPLE

Many of the insights of the saint stem from his experience as a sinner.

—Eric Hoffer

What distinguishes religious ethics from philosophical ethics is not so much a difference in the methods, or in the profoundness of the solutions, but in the basic content. The distinction, like that distinction that exists between denominations, is one of assumptions. The different assumptions reflect the different building blocks, the visions, the sacredness of their experience. George Thomas writes:

In brief, there is no such thing as an ethic which has been developed by pure reason without the aid of presuppositions. The difference between Christian ethics and secular moral philosophy is not that the former has presuppositions while the latter is free from them: it is that they derive their presuppositions from different sources.[1]

June O'Connor gives a different perspective:

To love other people in a sustained, deep, and generous way because one believes that God is real and has called all persons to a destiny of communion with him and with one another is a rational choice based on a particular view of the world. To love other people in a sustained, deep, and generous way simply because that in itself is better than living a life which gives primacy to self-concerns is also a rational choice rooted in a different world view.[2]

The religious perspective is one in which the experience and the response to the experience both suggest an ultimate source. There are many ways to respond to this, but two of the most common are called *normative* and *descriptive*. The *normative* approach reflects the idea that persons involved in the experience speak directly from their experience. They speak of their ethical experience in the same manner they speak of a spiritual experience. The second view, *descriptive*, reflects the understanding of the person whose involvement may not have been personal. Rather, their awareness of an ultimate experience is through the process of making ethical decisions which, in the main, reflect the ultimate source.[3]

In both cases the ultimate referred to is the presence of God. In the larger understanding the reference to God may mean the God of the RLDS Church as this God is understood through the teachings of Jesus Christ. Or it could be the experience of Buddha or the Universal Self. In every case the attachment is to the "ultimate other" which is the source of our "ultimate concern." It is this attachment which distinguishes these *particular* experiences from our daily routine and makes them principles or standards for behavior.

Religious ethics flows naturally from the human perspective that emerges from this ultimate concern. The ethic reflects a whole dimension of life which is based on fuller, richer, and more harmonious convictions. It acknowledges the necessity of giving meaning to the routines of our daily lives by allowing them to (perhaps making them) reflect the insights, values, and judgments of our religious understanding. What persons do in their religious ethical inquiry is to try to discover and identify

139

what common elements exist in their experience with the divine, and allow these common elements to become rules for human behavior. In some very important respects human beings have chosen not to violate the experience more than they have chosen not to violate any instructions the experience may have produced. It has been the case that while persons have not been very successful in bringing the end of fighting because God asked for peace, they have been surprisingly successful in agreeing not to fight in God's house.

Doing religious ethics requires a sensitive heart, a clear head, a defined method, an honest criticism, and a feel for discernment. It is concerned with an "ought," with an obligation or command. The source of information and the outcome of direction is judgment—a judgment more powerful and more eternal than any other. Religious ethics, then, has a wider application than rules or duty. For it deals with actions and laws that imply the need for human, as well as institutional, meaning in the presence of seemingly cold and calculated demands.[4]

Promptings

Ethical reflection is very common for religious persons. Alterations or adjustments in one's ethical point of view generally do not reflect the loss of faith or conversion from one faith to another. Rather, the changes, like the reflections, generally come into focus by virtue of the confusion which accompanies our attempts to live moral lives. On the surface it seems fairly simple to grant to Caesar what is his and to God what is God's. The confusion arises over who is in command, and what to do when it seems that Caesar wants what God demands or the other way around. Earlier we mentioned the dilemma of those who find themselves swearing to God that they will kill their country's enemies if necessary. When government says it has a right to speak in areas that seem to belong to God, or when one's convictions about divine intention lead one to civil disobedience, what is the answer?

Our individual responses require that we reason about these things. But eventually it will require even more. Because the moral life is more than reason, it is also mystical. It is an investigation of facts and rules and obligations; but it is also an investigation of virtues and values.

On the one hand, ethical inquiry that is primarily concerned with duty and obligation is called an *imperative* approach. Such an approach is concerned with supplying as set of rules or answers in response to questions about oughts, rights, and duties. These are pretty harsh and sometimes are designed to provide *the answer* to moral questions. For example, look at the current position taken by those who are afraid of sex education in public schools. Their answer to the increasing problem of AIDS and premarital sex is *DON'T*. That is probably a really good idea. However, it provides an answer rather than helping determine behavior.

Another approach is called *indicative*. It is concerned with seeking out values and virtue that lie behind any commands or directions. This approach seeks out the undone, is attuned to the unexpressed, and pays tribute to the uncommanded. Those using it ask not so much what ought I to do, but what *might* I do? They are not so much concerned with identifying that which is unethical as they are in seeing the ethical connotations of what

141

has not been accomplished. This is a broader—I am inclined to say more realistic—way of looking at ethics.

In the larger sense it seems that religious ethics is—and has more traditionally been—interested in indicative ethical approaches. But religious ethics is not without its imperative approaches and, as is often the case, those who believe this way tend to be more willing to state their case as a command than those seeking a more indicative manner. The loudness of the argument tells us more about those that argue, however, than it does the position that they hold.

Environment

One's ethical approach is greatly affected by the environmental background from which they look. This is probably more true for religious ethics than secular ethics. When I first started my undergraduate schooling, I remember with some clarity the requirement that I take a science course. I selected astronomy. The early phases of the course were spent discussing the nature of the telescope that we used. I came to understand that each instrument has its own history and that things are different because of individual and unique distortions caused in the making or the hanging of the telescope. In order to understand what it is that we were going to see through the telescope, we had first to learn the distortions of the scope itself. So it is with a look at our ethical understandings.

It is probably sufficient, before we begin the process of looking at the meaning of life, just to draw your attention to the fact that we are already the owners of some very strong assumptions about the meaning of life. The difficulty of being human is that we are partially made before we begin the process of making ourselves. We are already molded by specific religious and ethical traditions before we begin to look at ethical possibilities.

It generally has been assumed by religious as well as secular philosophers that persons of all cultures and backgrounds ask basically the same questions. This appears to be true. Persons tend to be alike despite differences in breeding, culture, and ability. They tend to have much the same needs and desires. The questions that arise from those needs and desires will differ some because of who they are, where they live, or the economic or social conditions under which they function. But sooner or later persons tend to find themselves involved in what philosophy has identified as the "perennial questions." These include questions about life and death, war and peace, duty and rights, and about responsibilities. They will ask serious questions about the nature of persons: who and what persons belong to, what persons are supposed to do if they are supposed to do anything special. All these questions tend to sound alike, address the same reality, seek out the same metaphysic, and often locate the same sort of answers.

Having said this it is still true that the way the questions are asked, the methods used to deal with the questions, and the answers arrived at, all reflect the beginning culture of the one asking. The duties which emerge from a highly structured civilization—as the Hindu—will be a much different set of duties than those that might emerge from a basically democratic people—like Americans. The degree to which the culture sees its citizens as individualistic—as in Christianity—will determine a different answer than a society or order that is primarily community based. In the same way one would expect a different set of answers from a highly religious country like Italy and a primarily secular country like Sweden.[5]

One of the most concerned and insightful writers on religious ethics today is June O'Connor. She suggests that being engaged in religious ethics is to be involved in a task composed of three aspects: concrete, theological, and epistemological. The tasks, as she defines them, are as follows.

1. Concrete-experiential level: This is the level at which we deal with conflicting claims for our attention and behavior. It is also the level at which values appear paradoxical. This is the most obvious and most used level of ethical consideration. It addresses itself to problems which are pressing and immediate and it is the point at which we rise from the confusion to take a stand. It has several steps of its own:

    a. Collecting the empirical data necessary to make a decision

    b. Seeking all the wisdom available by taking seriously principles, historical understandings, feelings, and sentimentality

    c. Anticipating the future implications of actions which we consider, realizing the impact of time as well as other actions in expanding our understanding

    d. Keeping in mind the distinction between adhering to the moral norm (like justice) and the means used to bring about the desire (like a revolution)

2. Theological-philosophical level: This is the

level at which we examine the interpretive frame-work discussed in level one. It is at this point that one's fundamental attitudes about life and the universe come into play. This sort of thinking requires

a. persons to realize the extent to which they are free agents;
b. to acknowledge that the historical community has shaped their thinking; and,
c. to lift up for self-criticism the convictions and the presuppositions of the past.

3. Epistemological level: This is the level at which we examine the methods by which we claim to know and to understand the philosophical and the theological. If we were doing this properly we would begin at the third level and work our way back to the first. However, that is generally not the case. It seems to be the nature of humans that they begin with what they consider to be concrete. In time that starts them to wondering about the theoretical. And after they see the theoretical more clearly they begin to wonder about the means by which they knew the concrete.[6]

The most significant part of what O'Connor has to say, I believe, is at this third level—the epistemological one—where she identifies our need for more understanding. If we do not know how we know, if we do not understand by what means we arrive at our understanding, then we have given in to traditions and cultural inclinations more than we need to.

But, of course, ethics is not just a rational event. The concept of emotion is significant within the ethical struggle as well. June O'Connor has something significant to say about this as well.

The discipline of religious ethics is intimately involved with and singularly expressive of the rhythm of life itself as this characterizes those who live reflectively. For ethical inquiry and reflection are rooted in the natural rhythms of doing and thinking and doing with new insight, of acting and analyzing and acting again.[7]

Each of us involved in thinking through the events of our lives and reflecting on our response to life is involved in a process of passions. We think, like we act, out of passion just as we do out of commitment. We think and we act—out of love and hate, out of fear and concern, out of dread and anguish. Critical reason is a process by which the free voice of calm can be directed toward that passion and allow it to cool. It helps us establish a common ground for passionate persons to talk and think less passionately. Nothing here is intended to suggest that one lose all passion, all emotion, or all commitment. No one would suggest such a thing out of ethical concern, only that such passion be at home with reason.

The Divine Command

Probably the oldest ethical theory is known as theological voluntarism or the divine command theory. It holds that the sole standard for the judgment of right and wrong is the law of God. An action or an event is right if God commanded it, wrong if he did not. Assuming that God is good, it easily follows that what is in his best interest is in our best interest. Whenever we can we should try and be like God. But whatever we do, it is imperative that we do what he says.[8]

While primarily religious, this approach is also secular in the sense that it serves as an outside command. It has the effect of judging utilitarian approaches just as any outside force judges an event by the act itself. It serves also to find fault with humanistic ethics. The divine command theory leaves no room for criteria, consequence, law, or goodness. Rather, it sees the command as the essence of morality. Truth and goodness are found only in obedience.

There were early suggestions that one could modify the commands of God by principles outlined in God's essence—that somehow universals and absolutes could replace obedience. But that failed to alter this point of view and led to a kind of idealism.

Early in my own philosophical training I ran across a word game that turned out to be very helpful for me. The question was this: "Is God good, or is what God does good because he does it?" It sounds like someone playing games, doesn't it? But it is making a good point. If God himself conforms to a standard that is good—that is, if God is to be judged against good—then good is more powerful (or at least is more independent) than God. On the other hand if God's actions are termed to be good—that is, good is what God does—then God and good are the same thing. In the divine command theory there is no abstract of good for it does not exist independently of God. C. F. Henry, who is one of those philosophical defenders of divine command theory, suggests that "intrinsic good" is alien to biblical theology for the God of the Bible reveals morality as his will.

Therefore, C. F. Henry wrote, "the good must be conceived in wholly personal dimensions. The good-in-itself is none other than God-in-himself. The good is what God wills and what he freely wills."[9]

The primary ethical stance has been that morality and religion are basically independent—at least, logically independent—and that it is not possible to base any morality on a religion. This argument is far too subtle and complicated for us to go into it very far here. The only point in raising the question is to indicate that when one separates morality from God's commands and places the ethical decision in human hands the question has changed from about how to *be* right to how to *do* right. *Being* right implies that what one does in mimicry of God is right by virtue of that mimicry. On the other hand, *doing* right suggests that by consideration of God's actions (Bible, etc.) we can determine what it is that he wants us to do, and do it. This makes us *doing* what is right (thus right is independent) rather than *being* right (right includes us). Think about this for a minute before you let it go.

Directly associated with the divine command idea is another point of view suggested by Emil Brunner. This is the source of the phrase "the divine imperative."

In the Christian view, that alone is "good" which is free from all caprice, which takes place in unconditional obedience. There is no Good save obedient behavior, save the obedient will.[10]

Thus Brunner agrees that the will of God cannot be established or totally explained by any principle. Even love is not a principle and every attempt we might make to see love as a principle further distorts it.

The Good consists simply and solely in the fact that man receives and deliberately accepts his life as a gift from God, as life dependent on "grace," as a gift, as the state of "being justified" because it has been granted as "justification by faith." Only thus can we know the Will of God, that is, in this revelation of Himself in which He manifests Himself as disinterested, generous Love. . . .[11]

148

Ethics in the divine imperative is that we should accept one thing: that we should live in God's love. He brings this message in the life of Christ and expands it apostolically in the freedom between mysticism and morality; there is no other virtue than the life of Love.

Quiz

Place the letter suggesting the proper match in the space provided before each sentence.

_____ 1. The term used to describe religious experience which is not personal.

_____ 2. Religious ethics is associated with the "ought" or _____.

_____ 3. The ethical approach primarily concerned with rules and duties.

_____ 4. The term used to describe religious experience that is personal.

_____ 5. Those ultimate questions that seem to be around in every generation.

_____ 6. The level at which one looks at the methods by which we know.

_____ 7. The ethical approach which seeks values rather than commands.

_____ 8. Also known as theological voluntarism.

A. Normative
B. Command
C. Perennial problems
D. Imperative
E. Epistemological
F. Divine Command
G. Descriptive
H. Indicative
I. Theological level

End Notes

1. As quoted in June O'Connor, "On Doing Religious Ethics" *Journal of Religious Ethics*, Vol. 7, No. 1 (Spring 1979), 88.
2. O'Connor, 91.
3. O'Connor, 82.
4. O'Connor, 92.
5. O'Connor, 82–83.
6. Levels based on O'Connor, 82–86.
7. O'Connor, 87.
8. William K. Frankena and John Glenrose, *Introductory Reading in Ethics* (New Jersey: Prentice–Hall, Inc., 1974), 94.
9. C. F. Henry, "The Good as the Will of God" in Frankena, *Readings*, 97.
10. As quoted in Frankena, *Readings*, 202–203.
11. Frankena, *Readings*, 203.

A DIFFERENT VIEW . . . GOLDEN RULE

The Golden Rule

Confucianism: What you don't want done to yourself, don't do to others.
—Sixth Century B.C.

Buddhism: Hurt not others with that which pains yourself.
—Fifth Century B.C.

Jainism: In happiness and suffering, in joy and grief, we should regard all creatures as we regard our own self, and should, therefore, refrain from inflicting upon others such injury as would appear undesirable to us if inflicted upon ourselves.
—Fifth Century B.C.

Zoroastrianism: Do not do unto others all that which is not well for yourself.
—Fifth Century B.C.

Classical Paganism: May I do to others as I would that they should do unto me.
—Fourth Century B.C.

Hinduism: Do naught to others which if done to thee would cause thee pain.
—Mahabharata, Third Century B.C.

Judaism: What is hateful to yourself, don't do to your fellow man.
—Rabbi Hillel, First Century B.C.

Christianity: Whatsoever ye would that men should do to you, do ye even so to them.
—Jesus, First Century C.E.

Sikhism: Treat others as thou wouldst be treated thyself.
—Sixteenth Century C.E.

CHAPTER 9

CHRISTIAN ETHICS AND RLDS ETHICAL ATTITUDES

*Judge not unrighteously, that ye be not judged;
but judge righteous judgment. For with what
judgment ye shall judge, ye shall be judged; and
with what measure ye mete, it shall be measured
to you again.*

—Matthew 7:2–3 IV

Christian Ethics

The principles of living which we acknowledge under the heading Christian ethics reflect no particular denominational understanding or theological conceptions—other than the fact one starts with a belief in the love of God and the healing ministry of Jesus Christ. Jesus made it abundantly clear that one could not rise to the heights of moral stability simply by obedience to rules. Rather, true ethical behavior is possible when persons inwardly accept and reflect that which God requires. Followers of this ethic often act as if God was establishing rules to be followed or goals to be accomplished. Christian behavior was not to be found in rules. The paradox probably results from the fact that the goals Christ suggested are not nearly so clear, or so easily followed, as are the rules ascribed to him. The God that Jesus suggests we follow—rather than simply obey—was, nevertheless, the same God who issued many commandments. In the next few pages we will talk about some of the implications of the
152

Christian ethic as traditionally established.

Christian ethics claims to be different from classical or modern ethics in the sense that it arises from divine revelation rather than from human reason or social experience. In effect, it is the moral teachings of the New Testament as expanded, altered, and expressed through centuries of dialogue. Because we assume God would only order what is good, then in following divine orders we have the advantage of our status as God's creatures. That creation is the beginning of our wisdom. In addition, we are guided by the knowledge of the moral history of humankind as reflected in the scriptures. This, like revealed truth, is expanded through the experience of the religious community (often the church) in which persons of goodwill are brought together by the power of the divine presence. And, finally, the guidelines for Christian ethics are to be found in the teachings of church leaders who have helped bring eternal truths into our realm of understanding.

Christian ethics was articulated early and given some systematic understanding by Augustine, bishop of Hippo Regius. Augustine felt the natural and only proper study for the human mind, as well as the proper goal for human desire, was God. It is to be understood from Augustine that both the love of God and the knowledge of God are gifts of divine grace. Knowledge is available through "faith seeking understanding." The truth available makes it possible for persons to move out of the wretchedness of their own lives and find joy in communion with their creator. Moral insight, therefore, is faith expressing itself in understanding.

Thomas Aquinas who lived some 800 years later is

153

usually seen as responsible for identifying Christian ethics in terms of virtue. Basing his ideas on Aristotle, Aquinas identified fortitude, temperance, liberality, magnificence, magnanimity, love of honor, gentleness, friendship, truthfulness, wittiness, and justice as the basic virtue. It is toward these virtues that the soul of a person moves in the process of actualization: that process in which a person is called to completion by the divine spark that is within. On the other hand, the body of a person (the flesh) is the appetite which seeks to fulfill the immediate desire. Ethical action results in the decision to respond to the soul rather than to the appetite. Persons incorporate the Christian ethic when they have arrived at the point in which virtue is exercised habitually—when persons *will* to be virtuous out of habit.

In both Augustine and Aquinas the concept of grace and divine illumination has carried the moral argument beyond what reason can determine. It introduces the mystical—the divine—as the source. The effect of this mystical understanding is found in community. Modern Christian ethics reflects the late Reformation's conception of a moral community. The community is the mechanism of justice which transforms the particular desires of competing interests and groups into benevolence as a principle of action. The result is a sense of justice which accepts community values and restricts individual desires.

The modern theme, mostly identified with Reinhold Niebuhr, calls out for a new relevance of the gospel of love and rejection of the secular culture. Opposed to the assumptions of ''liberal Christianity and its suggestions that people can satisfy the demands of love on their own, modern Christianity sees persons as creatures of both necessity and freedom.''[1] Humans are not capable of a full response to the demands of love, for the full response ''requires the transcendental virtues of grace and faith.''[2] Through grace persons become aware of the possibility of living life in agreement with God's will. And in faith, the possibility of realizing human good is materialized.

People are often at variance with themselves. They live in the opposing tendencies of exalted altruism and demonic selfishness. In a democracy one might see an example of the destructive nature of individualism (selfishness) versus the paternalism and potential creativity of mass expression (altruism). Niebuhr's moral philosophy argues for the ''relevance of the ideal of love in transcending all parochialism and egotism, to the demands of individual and social existence.''[3] The ideal of love is the only force which can correct the human tendency of destruction.

Christian ethics then is a moral proposition which holds that human good can only be understood in terms of ultimate goodness—free of all limitations, of all contingencies: a divine goodness. Like Plato's good, this good is independent of the desires of those who seek it as well as being independent of any temporal limitations which exemplify it. ''Moral goodness and happiness are attainable only through divine grace.''[4] As an ethic the principles of moral behavior are definable as ''rules'' and ''consequences,'' but they are in effect attitudes.

Behavior

Let us take a look at some of these principles of

Christian ethics that are available.

1. Underlying all such principles is obedience to God through the understandings provided by Jesus Christ. To ask "What am I to do?" and to regard "The will of God" as a reply is to ignore both what God is doing in the world and our own human situation. As well, it ignores the paradoxical character of the human situation: "We do not know the will of God which we will and we do not will the will of God which we know."[5] The more desperately persons seek to know the will of God, the more clearly they uncover what they both know and do not know, both will and do not will to do, that which they understand. The person who honestly responds to the direction, "Whoever of you does not renounce all that he has cannot be my disciple" is being obedient to the will of God. The radical nature of this renunciation is the beginning of the dissolution of the ethical paradox. It is the beginning of obedience.

2. Associated with this is the protection of rights provided to individuals on the basis of their creation. When we understand that persons have rights inherent in the fact of their creation, it enables us to respond to them in light of their personal dignity. We can never assume that others, because they are others, are less worthy; nor can we assume that others' freedom is either a restriction on our own or a commodity for which we can bargain. Perhaps we can only acknowledge the dignity and independence of others. But this acknowledgment is necessary if we are to treat—and be treated—as our creator wills.

3. A third requirement is the acknowledgment of goals which, as Christians, we must establish if we
156

are to live our lives reminiscent of Jesus Christ who died for us. Assuming the goal of a loving world, we are prone to recognize that acts of love are the most important behavioral acts. Such an assumption accepts an act or behavior as being right (good) only if it is an act of love. It recognizes, of course, that acts are loving or not depending on the consequence. But it leaves open to our determination the question if an act *can be* loving, if the consequences of the act are not loving.

4. A fourth principle asserts that Christians seek a better world—a kingdom of God. Their search is motivated by realizing that the living of a good life here on earth is indicative of a better life anticipated to be lived in the kingdom, in God's world. This principle assumes humans are moving toward perfection via stepping stones representing levels of the perfect.

5. A fifth manner in which the Christian ethic is identified as a principle is in the context. That is, Christian ethics grows out of the context of our love. Our response to God's love calls us to consider the loving situation. It asks, ''What would Jesus do?'' Having decided—because of love not because of rules or duties or obligations or the expectation of certain consequences—we then act in this love.

6. A final principle to be identified is the establishment of norms of behavior. By norms I am referring to standards established through years of tradition, as well as through interpretation of the scriptures and the directions of Christian leaders. These norms include such things as peace, commitment, security, love, reasonableness, responsibility, community, obedience, and covenant. Human beings seeking relief from their failures and from the

chaos and unpredictability of their worlds are anxious to behave in a manner that meets the norms of their creator. They know they cannot live forever in the guilt of unaccomplished kindness. They seek to be kind to the degree of kindness they see in God's love. They have a standard against which to measure, a vision against which all individual dreams are checked. We use these norms as a means of evaluation and definition. Often we express our standards in terms of rules, values, virtues, rights, and goodness.

RLDS Ethical Theories

It is extremely difficult to put together any principles of ethical behavior that might be distinctive within the RLDS movement. Obviously this does not mean the RLDS are not ethical people. Quite the contrary, it means there has been no systematic analysis or description of such an ethic. Because of the primary Christianity of the church, I am sure there really are few distinctives which would apply to the RLDS exclusively. Some years ago a friend was trying to explain to me that science is not always some identifiable body of knowledge but is often what persons with a scientific mind seek to understand. In desperation he said: ''Science is what scientists do!'' In the same manner RLDS ethical behavior is what ethical RLDS people do. Having said this, however, there are, nevertheless, some things worth pointing out about RLDS principles and ethics.

We can assume to a limited degree that the RLDS people hold to a ''divine imperative'' ethic. There is a strong belief that God decides ethical behavior. The fact that the church believes in continuing

158

revelation would seem to mean that the RLDS people have the ethical advantage of continued, and thus modern, sources of behavioral determination.

On the other hand, RLDS people have a strong sense of agency and are not easily led in such things as ethical standards. The church as an institution has been reluctant to take a strong stand in some areas of modern ethical dilemmas, preferring instead to stress underlying principles and recognize the individual's need for decision-making.

Certainly a large measure of RLDS people would fall under the umbrella of Christian ethics. And having this assumption, plus the assumption of membership and priesthood responsibility, we might well point out the high degree of accountability present. This is a contextual point of view. Barbara Higdon, writing for a church committee on ethics, said:

The steward is responsible both to God and to his or her fellow humans in the decision-making process. Also, the impact of personal decisions on the larger communities of which one is a member provides a further context for those decisions. All of the foregoing concepts are extensions of life of the principles of love of God and love of neighbor which provide the primary context for Christian ethics. A significant affirmation of the Restoration is that God's will is continuously revealed to responsive persons. Ethically this implies that human choice and behavior are perceived as responses to God's action in our lives. Being responsive necessarily includes our living as disciples in community with God, on the one hand, and our fellow humans on the other. Living in Christian community means living responsively and responsibly with others under God's prevailing grace, taking into account the full measure of our personhood.[6]

Some Moral Responses:

On January 4, 1973, the First Presidency addressed a meeting of nearly 200 appointees and

World Church ministers. The occasion was a significant one and addressed the ethical demands of their common calling. In it they addressed principles which would be manifested in moral behavior. They were seeking some larger understanding of basic demands of ministers of the church.[7] Among these principles the Presidency offered an identification of a hierarchy of obligations:

1. First, to "be loyal to our understanding of the nature of God and of the universe and of humankind." This call for loyalty expressed the church's need to recognize individual members' understanding of the nature of God in their lives, as well as their understanding of the meaning of the universe in which they must operate. In addition it stressed the need to be loyal to our own individual assurances of the nature of humankind. All ethical behavior starts there.

2. Second, the members assembled were called to be loyal to the "institutional expressions of the divine purpose." While the church is pluralistic in its understandings, we have accepted the fact that the institutional church, because of its prophetic leadership and community consent, is the best source of understanding of God's plan and expression.

3. The third obligation is a loyalty to our own specific "roles within those institutions." It is important to recognize the various roles we play and to acknowledge that in the course of our lives we are called upon to play many such roles. Sometimes we are leader, sometimes follower. Some roles will require special talents, some special callings, but all are roles designed to bring out the best from our potential and to serve the church as an institution.

Therefore, in each and every case we must perform to the very best of our ability.

4. The Presidency also called for loyalty to the particular tasks prescribed by these assigned roles. Such a sense of loyalty at first draws us to the fact that we are obligated to perform the tasks asked of us. But obviously it means more than that. It is a call to perform at the very best of our ability, to bring to bear every talent that we have, to give the work the time and effort needed to accomplish the purpose, and to give to the assignment the full measure of devotion necessary.

In their presentation the members of the Presidency acknowledged conflicts will sometimes develop among these obligations. The ethical person is often called upon to make decisions about which of these demands conflict. The expectations of one situation often seem to run against a person's understandings of the role or even to run counter to an understanding of the nature of God. What do we do in terms of our behavior and attitude when our personal understanding is different, perhaps even in direct confrontation, with that of the institutional leadership?

Such conflict may arise from differences in information or failure to understand procedures or being unaware of prior commitments. Thus one's first ethical duty would be to maintain as much humility as possible while discovering whether one is dealing with fundamental issues of doctrine or moral responsibility. Or perhaps, the disagreement is just a difference in opinion or of taste. Such a person must also give consideration to the priority of obligations, to higher and lower values, and to what moral precedence there might be. It will be rarely

161

true—if indeed we are in the same organization and have arrived at basically the same understandings—that one person will find oneself in too deep a conflict with another. However, there are some deep disagreements within the increasing pluralism of the RLDS Church. And if that is the cause of the conflict, what then?

How do we resolve such ethical problems? The Presidency's article outlines "certain steps...required by our moral philosophy." They are:

1. As ethical persons we must remember that our colleagues have at least as much integrity as we do. The persons with whom we deal are as concerned about the church as are we and concerned as well at doing what they consider to be God's will. There is the old joke about the two ministers fighting over the truths of their respective beliefs. Finally, in an assumed gesture of peace, one said: "Why do we fight? We are both trying to do God's will. You in your way. I in God's way." We must avoid any such assumption. Just because we disagree does not prove any lack of integrity on another's part.

2. As ethical persons we must make every effort to obtain all the facts possible prior to our decision. To make our stand on the basis of limited or potentially wrong information is by that fact alone to be acting unethically. When such information is not available to us it is necessary for us to suspend judgment and avoid the temptation to arrive at premature decisions.

3. In matters of official decisions and responsibility, it is important to recognize the difference between mutual dedication to the cause and personally opposing views. Again, we are called to be sure of ourselves and to recognize that personal

opinion is not necessarily doctrinal truth.

4. The right of free opinion and discussion is not designed, nor does it provide, license to frustrate the will of the body as expressed through World Conference. The will of the majority, acting in Conference assembled, and recognized as common consent rather than as democracy, is final. That is the nature as well as the theological base of the church institution. Ethical persons will be aware and responsive to this fact.

5. Unity within the institution is a matter of mutual respect within our pluralism rather than identicalness of thought or total acceptance of any of the many interpretations of doctrine. Consent does not necessarily mean you agree or that you like the decision. It means that you accept it and that your opinion—whatever it may be—will not be used against the body.

6. Ethical people will recognize the church as an instrument of growth and accept that growth often must begin with the recognition we might have been wrong. If there is no change in insight or growth, then there is neither revelation nor hope. We must expect our past and our present (thus our future) to be in conflict over some issues.

Stewardship Ethics

As we have stressed several times thus far, ethics are principles of (for) moral behavior. As principles they reflect not just one or two behaviors but the underlying guidelines or assumptions of all moral life. Such an ethic reflects clear-cut goals and patterns which, in the case of the Christian ethicists, reflect the examples of Jesus as Savior. Within the RLDS movement the "cause of Zion" has been an important part of the development of the ethical principles we can identify. Our revelation, our tradition, and our community understanding all tend to be directed to this urgent task. To a large measure our behavior is affected by it. Roger Yarrington, writing on ethics some twenty-five years ago, said: "One cannot participate in Zionic endeavors without a fundamental relationship with God, which is reflected in our behavior. Latter Day Saints call this relationship, this outlook, this pattern of guidelines, 'stewardship.'"[8]

Underlying the cause of Zion are some basic theological and religious principles which emerge from our understandings of the scriptures. Primary among these are the following:

1. God is our creator (D. and C. 22:21). We mean by this that God is the source and the goal. God is the explanation for what is.

2. God creates persons with purpose and meaning, thus human life has both qualities. The acceptance of purpose suggests—in many cases, demands—a right way of living in order to accomplish that goal.

3. Our true calling is to the service of God. We are called to serve with all our might and with all our souls, such service including the use of material and spiritual possessions for this purpose.

4. We are stewards over the earth and over the things of our earth. There has been an increasing tendency, especially in the United States, to act as if the resources of this earth belonged to us for our immediate use and with no thought for tomorrow or those who will come after us. The cause of Zion would suggest that as stewards we must be responsible for the earth and its resources. We must use

164

them wisely or not at all and conserve all that we can for future generations. Ours is the responsibility to replenish what we can and to aid nature in its job of rebuilding that which we have used for our benefit.

5. Life is whole. We see life totally, not fragmented into spiritual and physical parts, nor do we divide the secular and the sacred or mine as against God's. Rather, humans are united consisting of mixtures and blends, all of which pull together in love. To be truly sacred is to see the sacred and the secular as one, to find God in our activities whatever they may be, and to take our experience with God into our vocation and into the world at large.

6. As persons responsible to God for the fact of our creation and for the use of that which was created with and for us, we are constantly aware of the revelation of what is expected of us. "In all thy ways acknowledge him and he shall direct thy paths" (Proverbs 3:6). As we become more and more assured of God's presence in our lives, the paths of righteousness and goodness become more clear.

What Now?

The obvious question, however, is what does this mean in terms of ethical behavior? What shall we do when the question of our behavior and our stewardship goals seem to be at odds with our desires and our feelings? Yarrington says: "Determination to be a good steward, if carried to its fullest extent, establishes the ethical guidelines needed to meet any problem."[9] Such a statement assures us of our mission; unfortunately, it does not help us decide what we should do. Over the years the church has

165

made some significant ethical statements; it has provided guidelines for its members in terms of moral questions that face the church and the world. While time alters both the approach and the responses to moral questions, the church often feels the need to establish a statement of the unity of feelings.

It will be helpful to mention some principles, and then look at some of the guidelines.

Principles

Over the years the RLDS Church has emphasized certain ethical principles which are reasonably consistent with the contextual view earlier discussed. Peter Judd and Bruce Lindgren identify some of these in *Introduction to the Saints Church.*[10] They are paraphrased here for consideration.

1. Each person has a special worth and uniqueness in the sight of God. This fundamental ethical principle is our response to the fact of our creation. Because we are all of special worth, nothing should be done to violate the rights and human dignity of *any* person.

2. Our personal ethics should be such that they allow us to serve God as fully as possible. This is reflective of the "Word of Wisdom" (Section 86) and asserts the need to maintain discipline according to the doctrines of the church and in response to the presence of the Holy Spirit.

3. Our participation would be directed toward building a society of peace, justice, and personal fulfillment for all persons.

166

Some Ethical Positions Taken

MARRIAGE

True marriage is a sacrament, and should not be entered into lightly, hastily, or unworthily.[11]

Marriage is a sacred covenant between husband and wife in which God participates with sanction, blessing, and guidance. The church is committed to providing premarital preparation and other caring ministries to strengthen and nurture faithful marriage relationships.

Marriage is sacred when it expresses the nature of God through the relationship of husband and wife. The marriage ceremony, when performed by the authority of the church, is intended to be a solemnization and public witness of the covenanting couple with God and is thus considered a sacrament. The marriage partners, and all others in the ceremony, should approach it with mature consideration and adequate preparation. They should expect that God will bless them in the fulfillment of their various responsibilities.

UNMARRIED PARENTS

The material which follows on unmarried parents and abortions is adapted from the *Church Administrators Handbook.*[12]

Premarital chastity is to be encouraged. Ministry given to a person involved in premarital sex should be directed toward repentance and reformation.

When pregnancy occurs outside of marriage and the wisdom of marriage is raised, the following facts should be kept in mind:

1. Christian marriage is intended as a life partnership based on mutual affection and respect and on

the fundamental Christian character of the parties. If such a basis for marriage exists, marriage is generally advisable. But if no such basis exists, marriage should not be advised just because of the pregnancy.

2. The welfare of the child conceived by the parties should be given major consideration in light of the specific circumstances. This consideration should include such matters as the legal status of the child, financial support, and prospective home situation after birth.

3. An equally major concern is the welfare of the parents. This includes the financial costs of the pregnancy but extends to the recovery of the parents to a stable life-style.

4. Each of the parties should be advised and helped to accept willingly the measure of responsibility which the total situation indicates.

5. Consultations should be arranged with appropriate social agencies.

ABORTION

The following conclusions were developed by a committee composed of physicians, social scientists, an attorney, and church officials:

1. We affirm our faith in God, and in the fellowship of the church, as the work of God among us. This faith provides the context within which decisions about abortion should be made.

2. We affirm our shared humanity and common need for redemption and reconciliation to God and to one another.

3. We affirm that parenthood is partnership with God in the creative processes of the universe.

4. We affirm the necessity for parents to make re-

sponsible decisions regarding the conception and nurture of their children.

5. We affirm a profound regard for the personhood of the woman in her emotional, mental, and physical health; we also affirm a profound regard and concern for the potential of the unborn fetus.

6. We affirm the inadequacy of simplistic answers that regard all abortions as murder, or, on the other hand, regard abortion only as a medical procedure without moral significance.

7. We affirm the right of the woman to make her own decision regarding the continuation or termination of problem pregnancies. Preferably this decision should be made in cooperation with her companion and in consultation with a physician, qualified minister, or professional counselor. This decision should be made in light of the full range of moral, medical, legal, and cultural influences within which the person lives.

8. We affirm the need for skilled counselors being accessible to the membership of the church to assist persons in their struggle with issues centering in human sexuality, responsible parenthood, and wholeness of family life. Church leaders need to be aware of counseling resources in the community to which our members may be referred.

HOMOSEXUALITY

The following material is from the policy adopted by the Standing High Council.[13] The issue of homosexuality is demanding increased attention in Western society today. Though the church is faced with changing attitudes about the existence and expression of homosexuality, it continues to hold to the norm of heterosexuality and exclusively sanctions heterosexual marriage. In doing so, the church recognizes that homosexual Christians and heterosexual Christians are all brothers and sisters and share in common the love and grace of God. In addition, the church is aware that anti-homosexual bias has long existed in Western cultures in general, and that homosexuals have been and still are denied social justice.

In light of the preceding, the following guidelines should be noted by administrative officials:

The church recognizes that there is a difference between homosexual orientation and homosexual activity (defined as sexual acts between persons of the same sex). The former is accepted as a condition over which a person may have little or no control; the latter is considered immoral and cannot be condoned by the church.

The church affirms the worth of all persons. Homosexuals as well as heterosexuals are children of God and have full claim upon the acceptance and reconciling ministry and care of the church. That is, individuals with a homosexual orientation who refrain from homosexual acts should be fully accepted into the ongoing life of the congregation. Those persons who engage in homosexual acts should be dealt with in terms of redemptive ministry and/or church law procedures in the same way as those who engage in heterosexual acts outside of marriage.

HUMAN RIGHTS

As members of the world community, the church has often voiced its appreciation for the Universal Declaration of Human Rights as approved by the General Assembly of the United Nations on December 10, 1948.[14] While never "approved" by the church it presents a response that has been widely accepted and, in lacking one of our own, is a wise model to consider.

Preamble

Whereas recognition of the inherent dignity and of the equal and inalienable rights of all members of the human family is the foundation of freedom, justice and peace in the world,

Whereas disregard and contempt for human rights have resulted in barbarous acts which have outraged the conscience of mankind, and the advent of a world in which human beings shall enjoy freedom of speech and belief and freedom from fear and want has been proclaimed as the highest aspiration of the common people.

Whereas it is essential, if man is not to be compelled to have recourse, as a last resort, to rebellion against tyranny and oppression, that human rights should be protected by the rule of the law,

Whereas it is essential to promote the development of friendly relations between nations,

Whereas the peoples of the United Nations have in the Charter reaffirmed their faith in fundamental human rights, in the dignity and worth of the human person and in the equal rights of men and women and have determined to promote social progress and better standards of life in larger freedom,

Whereas Member States have pledged themselves to achieve, in co-operation with the United Nations, the promotion of universal respect for and observation of human rights and fundamental freedoms,

Whereas a common understanding of these rights and freedoms is of the greatest importance for the full realisation of this pledge, NOW, THEREFORE, THE GENERAL ASSEMBLY proclaims

THIS UNIVERSAL DECLARATION OF HUMAN RIGHTS as a common standard of achievement for all peoples and all nations, to the end that every individual and every organ of society, keeping this Declaration constantly in mind, shall strive by teaching and education to promote respect for these rights and freedoms and by progressive measures, national and international, to secure their universal and effective recognition and observance, both among the peoples of Member States themselves and among the peoples of territories under their jurisdiction.

Article 1. All human beings are born free and equal in dignity and rights. They are endowed with reason and conscience and should act towards one another in a spirit of brotherhood.

Article 2. Everyone is entitled to all the rights and freedoms set forth in this Declaration, without distinction of any kind, such as race, colour, sex, language, religion, political or other opinion, national or social origin, property, birth, or other status.

Furthermore, no distinction shall be made on the basis of the political, jurisdictional or international status of the country or territory to which a person belongs, whether it be independent, trust, non-self-governing or under any other limitation of sovereignty.

Article 3. Everyone has the right to life, liberty, and security of person.

Article 4. No one shall be held in slavery or servitude; slavery and the slave trade shall be prohibited in all their forms.

Article 5. No one shall be subjected to torture or to cruel, inhuman or degrading treatment or punishment.

Article 6. Everyone has the right to recognition everywhere as a person before the law.

Article 7. All are equal before the law and are entitled without any discrimination to equal protection of the law. All are entitled to equal protection against any discrimination in violation to this Declaration and against any incitement to such discrimination.

Article 8. Everyone has the right to an effective remedy by the competent national tribunals for acts violating the fundamental rights granted him by the constitution or by law.

Article 9. No one shall be subject to arbitrary arrest, detention or exile.

Article 10. Everyone is entitled in full equality to a fair and public hearing by an independent and impartial tribunal, in the determination of his rights and obligations and of any criminal charge against him.

Article 11. (1) Everyone charged with a penal offence has the right to be presumed innocent until proved guilty according to law in a public trial at which he has had all the guarantees necessary for his defense.

(2) No one shall be held guilty of any penal offence on account of any act or omission which did not constitute a penal offence, under national or international law, at the time when it was committed. Nor shall a heavier penalty be imposed than the one that was applicable at the time the penal offence was committed.

Article 12. No one shall be subjected to arbitrary interference with his privacy, family, home or correspondence, nor to attacks upon his honour and reputation. Everyone has the right to the protection of the law against such interference or attacks.

Article 13. (1) Everyone has the right to freedom of movement and residence within the borders of each State.

(2) Everyone has the right to leave any country, including his own, and to return to his country.

Article 14. (1) Everyone has the right to seek and to enjoy another country's asylum from persecution.

(2) This right may not be invoked in the case of prosecutions genuinely arising from non-political crimes or from acts contrary to the purposes and principles of the United Nations.

Article 15. (1) Everyone has the right to a nationality.

(2) No one shall be arbitrarily deprived of his nationality nor denied the right to change his nationality.

Article 16. (1) Men and women of full age, without any limitation due to race, nationality or religion, have the right to marry and to found a family. They are entitled to equal rights as to marriage, during marriage and at its dissolution.

(2) Marriage shall be entered into only with the free and full consent of the intending spouses.

(3) The family is the natural and fundamental group unit of society and is entitled to protection by society and the State.

Article 17. (1) Everyone has the right to own property alone as well as in association with others.

(2) No one shall be arbitrarily deprived of his property.

Article 18. Everyone has the right to freedom of thought, conscience, and religion; this right includes freedom to change his religion or belief, and freedom, either alone or in community with others, and in public or private, to manifest his religion or belief in teaching, practice, worship and observance.

Article 19. Everyone has the right to freedom of opinion and expression; this right includes freedom to hold opinions with-

173

out interference and to seek, receive, and impart information and ideas through any media and regardless of frontiers.

Article 20. (1) Everyone has the right to freedom of peaceful assembly and association.

(2) No one may be compelled to belong to an association.

Article 21. (1) Everyone has the right to take part in the government of his country, directly or through freely chosen representatives.

(2) The will of the people shall be the basis of the authority of government; this will shall be expressed in periodic and genuine elections which shall be by universal and equal suffrage and shall be held by secret vote or by equivalent free voting procedures.

Article 22. Everyone, as a member of society, has the right to social security and is entitled to realisation, through national effort and international cooperation and in accordance with the organisation and resources of each State, of the economic, social and cultural rights indispensable for his dignity and the free development of his personality.

Article 23. (1) Everyone has the right to work, to free choice of employment, to just and favorable conditions of work, and to protection against unemployment.

(2) Everyone, without any discrimination, has the right to equal pay for equal work.

(3) Everyone who works has the right to just and favorable remuneration ensuring for himself and his family an existence worthy of human dignity, and supplemented, if necessary, by other means of social protection.

(4) Everyone has the right to form and to join trade unions for the protection of his interests.

Article 24. Everyone has the right to rest and leisure, including reasonable limitation of working hours and periodic holidays with pay.

Article 25. (1) Everyone has the right to a standard of living adequate for the health and well-being of himself and of his family, including food, clothing, housing and medical care and necessary social services, and the right to security in the event of unemployment, sickness, disability, widowhood, old age or other lack of livelihood in circumstances beyond his control.

(2) Motherhood and childhood are entitled to special care and assistance. All children whether born in or out of wedlock, shall

enjoy the same social protection.

Article 26. (1) Everyone has the right to education. Education shall be free, at least in the elementary and fundamental stages. Elementary education shall be compulsory. Technical and professional education shall be made generally available and higher education shall be equally accessible to all on the basis of merit.

(2) Education shall be directed to the full development of the human personality and to the strengthening of respect for human rights and fundamental freedoms. It shall promote understanding, tolerance and friendship among all nations, racial or religious groups, and shall further the activities of the United Nations for the maintenance of peace.

(3) Parents have a prior right to choose the kind of education that shall be given to their children.

Article 27. (1) Everyone has the right to freely participate in the cultural life of the community, to enjoy the arts and to share in scientific advancement and its benefits.

(2) Everyone has the right to the protection of the moral and material interests resulting from any scientific, literary or artistic production of which he is the author.

Article 28. Everyone is entitled to a social and international order in which the rights and freedoms set forth in this Declaration can be fully realized.

Article 29. (1) Everyone has duties to the community in which alone the free and full development of his personality is possible.

(2) In the exercise of his rights and freedoms, everyone shall be subject only to such limitations as are determined by law solely for the purpose of securing due recognition and respect for the rights and freedoms of others and of meeting the just requirements of morality, public order and the general welfare in a democratic society.

(3) These rights and freedoms may in no case be exercised contrary to the purposes and principles of the United Nations.

Article 30. Nothing in this Declaration may be interpreted as implying for any State, group or person any right to engage in any activity or to perform any act aimed at the destruction of any of the rights and freedoms set forth herein.

Quiz

Complete the following questions with information from the material in chapter 9:

1. Christian ethics is different from classical or modern ethics because:

2. The idea that knowledge is faith seeking understanding came from

3. The modern theme, usually identified with Reinhold Niebuhr, calls out for the:

4. Christ came to tell us about following more than about obeying. What does this mean in terms of ethics?

5. The RLDS tend to hold both to a _____ ethic and to accept the idea of agency.

6. What are the levels of loyalty that the First Presidency acknowledged in their 1973 statement?

End Notes

1. William A. Banner, *Ethics: An Introduction to Moral Philosophy* (New York: Charles Scribner's Sons, 1968), 89.
2. Banner, 89.
3. Banner, 91.
4. Banner, 92–93.
5. Paul L. Lehmann, *Ethics in a Christian Context* (New York: Harper and Row, 1963), 80.
6. Barbara Higdon, "A Community of Conviction," *Saints Herald*, Vol. 128 (April 1981), 26–28.
7. "Ethical Demands of Our Common Calling," *Saints Herald*, Vol. 120 (March 1973), 10–13.

8. Roger Yarrington, *Restoration Ethics Today* (Independence: Herald House, 1963), 161.
9. Yarrington, 165.
10. Peter Judd and Bruce Lindgren, *Introduction to the Saints Church* (Independence: Herald House, 1976), 198–200.
11. Adapted from the church's statement in General Conference Resolution 1182.
12. Herald House, 1987.
13. March 18, 1982.
14. Resolution 217 (III) A.

A CASE IN POINT . . . SOCIETY AND THE SINNER

It was Mark Twain who pointed out to newspaper reporters, when they asked if he was a member of a certain club, "I would not belong to a club that would have me as a member." Others have picked up on this theme, usually in the same humor, creating as they do a very interesting ethical question. I used to suggest to persons that "I was the sort of little boy my mother did not want me to play with"—again, partly in jest but with some real understanding of what is involved. Most of us who are involved in the Christian community—either at large or as members of a congregation—often find ourselves in a situation where we know we are not the sort of members we would like to be associated with.

How then can an organization dedicated to the love of Jesus Christ and concerned about persons, and which is composed of sinners, all of whom fall short of the expectations imposed by the organization, excommunicate persons?

Consider the following:

1. Is there such a thing as selective or priority evils?
2. Are confessed sins more destructive than unconfessed ones?

177

3. How can members of a church judge other members of the church?
4. At what point do the needs of the organization to appear ''good'' offset the needs of the persons to be accepted even if ''bad''?
5. What does membership suggest? What qualifies us to be members of organizations other than the characteristics of the other members?

CHAPTER 10

WHY IS IT SO HARD TO BE ETHICAL?

If you can assume with St. Paul, St. Augustine, Thomas Hobbes, John Calvin, and a number of other moral thinkers, that human beings are fundamentally and naturally selfish, what is to keep professionals from devouring their clients rather than helping them?

—Darrell Reeck

The answer to the quotation is, of course, that some professionals do spend their time devouring their clients. More and more of them are inclined in that manner. It is hard to be ethical. It is hard because being ethical pits the rewards of generalized behavior against the gratification of immediate behavior. And that is difficult for all of us. Maybe a good place to start in trying to decide why it is so hard to be ethical would be to look at what is now called professional ethics. Professional ethics is based on what used to be called the "ethics of character" and meant the ethics of obligation, aspiration, egoism, and commitment. It is called professional ethics because the ideas have been adapted in the past few decades by professions which are trying to take seriously what it means to be an ethical person in the modern world. Perhaps in this search we can find some early suggestions about what it means to be involved in the morality of aspiration.

179

Philosophers sometimes talk about the "art of ethics," meaning the act of reflecting on the moral dimensions of one's behavior—in this case of one's work. Professional ethics, then, is often considered an "art because it is more related to the reflection than it is to the addressing of particular problems." It is different from any "code" of conduct that might be adopted by a particular profession or social organization. The Lions Club Code of Ethics for social or professional organizations is really membership requirements and reflects neither on what is being acknowledged as a principle nor how one behaves.

Why?

It is not going to come as too great a surprise to you that most philosophers have not been able to answer this question directly. They have, however, pointed out that the nature of the question itself may give you your first answer. Let us look at one or two of these philosophical inquiries prior to providing some answers—however limited—on our own.

F. H. Bradley in his *Ethical Studies* points out that in asking the question, "Why should I be moral?" we are really asking, "Of what good is it?" or maybe "For what is it good?" Such questions assume that nothing (at least morality) is good in itself. It assumes something is good only when it is a means to an end. Good means good for us. It would appear that morality—at least to someone asking the question in the above manner—is a means to an end and not an end in itself. By virtue of the question, *ipso facto,* the questing person does not accept virtue as the end and, therefore, has answered his own ques-
180

tion. "You should be good to accomplish the end that virtue will provide."

It is the same as asking "What advantage will morality give me?" To say virtue is to suggest that it "transcends all the possible delights of vice."[1] But that is not what is being asked. So we ask Bradley: Does asking why one should be moral make any sense at all? His answer is "no." If morality is an end in itself, you do not need to ask the question. If it is not an end in itself, then the question is not about morality but about whatever the end is you are seeking. Obviously, if the end is of value then the means to arrive at it will be valuable as well.

Another point of view about the question is provided by P. H. Nowell-Smith.[2] When a person asks, "Why does a person obey a rule at a particular occasion," Nowell-Smith says the question can be answered threefold: (1) He may want to do that particular thing regardless of any reason, and (2) he may act out of force of habit, or (3) he may act out of motive. When a person acts out of a motive it is usually one of the following:

• Hypothetical imperative: seeing it as the best way to achieve what he wants to achieve.

• Sanction: believing that she has reason to be afraid of the consequences if she fails.

• Conform: desire to conform to the codes of his society, to fit in, and to do the right thing.

• Desire: she may decide to obey rules; when those rules happen to be moral ones, it is called moral duty.

But let us ask a somewhat different question with the same intent. "Why are there any rules at all?" Perhaps there are two ways to deal with the question suggested in this manner.

1. Harmonious life: We have rules because everyone has a variety of aims in life and they cannot all be fully achieved because they will on some occasions conflict with each other. If a person is to pursue "long-term interests satisfactorily he must curb his passions."[3] To live a harmonious life one has a rule to prevent them from being in a constant state of confrontation.

2. Social harmony: We have rules because they are necessary to enable persons to cooperate successfully in actions which logically or practically they are unable to conduct alone. Or perhaps to settle the disputes that would result from the anarchy of persons having different opinions.

Another response to the question "Why should I be moral?" is because of the imperatives of character, obligation, aspiration, egoism, and commitment. Let's look at each of these for a minute.

Ethics of Character

The ethics of character refers to that aspect of persons which understands their naked self-interest must be balanced with loving service to the community in which they make their home. And that this control must in fact change vice to virtue in a manner which will transform persons. It is often expressed within the confines of professional ethics because of the fact the role of the professional is one where the temptation to exploit is high because of ability and specialization.

Thus character ethics is concerned with the development of the good in persons. It recommends a virtue based on the standard Greek traditions: justice, prudence, temperance, and courage. The theological (philosophical) minded among them have added faith, hope, and love.

Let us use justice as one example. In the professions it may well be concerned with the fair distributions of price and rewards. Justice here would mean charging everyone the same and granting benefits equally. In terms of more significant things like freedom, it is the assurance that all are called on to pay the high cost of freedoms enjoyed and that all share equally in the freedom. In terms of prudence, this concept assumes the necessity of giving regard to one's own welfare while taking care not to misuse one's self in the struggle for community value. Temperance requires all to take and to give in moderation, never committed to one thing at the exclusion of all others. And courage—some consider it to be the cardinal virtue—is the ability to face danger for the sake of principle. It is the courage to be one's self in the presence of demands for intemperance, imprudence, and injustice that is often the test of real ethics.

Faith is the acceptance that what one suspects about reality is true and acknowledging that whatever proof there is concerning source and expectation lies outside of our own minds. We believe because we have faith. Usually this means faith in God, but in a larger sense it also means faith to accept the unseen as real and faith to live in the confidence of one's knowledge. Hope, on the other hand, is the promise of the unseen future which—in the midst of the absurdities of the world—promises better, more significant, days. And love, despite its thousands of meanings and legions of distortions, is the willingness to give one's self for another. Such love is to be found "in the enlargement of one's personal boundaries to facilitate the achievement of personal wholeness by other human beings."[4]

Ethics of Obligation

The ethics of obligation asserts that one must respond to the stated principles of moral laws. This view depends on seeing moral laws as scientific principles. It is an ethic of duty and obligation and is generally found among institutionalized ethics, religions, and philosophical schools.

This ethics of obligation is based on the Kantian maxim that any action you accept must be judged against your willingness to see the proposed action made a universal law. The steps necessary in using this maxim of social behavior are simple.

1. Clarify what the action is that you are considering.
2. State the underlying rule indicated by the nature of the behavior.
3. Universalize the idea—make it a law to be obeyed by all persons.
4. Determine if the universal law you have envisioned is inconsistent or self-contradictory.
5. Determine if you would be willing to obey such a law.

The obvious purpose is to see the full implications of your immediate action taken to its logical conclusions. This "categorical imperative" has the advantage of great consistency and the ease of providing definite actions for definite crimes or misbehaviors. And it lays stress on doing what is right, or correct, or one's duty for its own sake.

Ethics of Aspiration

Aspiration is a more acceptable word among hard-nosed professionals than theological ones. It means ethics based on goals or ends. Here one seeks to aspire—that is, desires—to act in a manner which produces a better state of qualitative affairs.

It depends a great deal, as you can see, on what one aspires to. The goals of our aspirations are legion and will fill the pages not only of ethics books but ones on metaphysics and reality concepts. Among these is the well-known concept of J. S. Mill and his followers. It is called utilitarianism and suggests one acts for the greatest amount of good for the greatest (largest) number of people within the community. By good, utilitarians generally mean happiness or well-being. It is important, however, to recognize Mill is not talking about pleasure but deep-seated happiness. Such a point of view drives one to the consideration of every member of—or at least the majority members of—the community.

It is often pointed out that such a view is unworkable because it is just as difficult for the community to know the greatest or the best as it is for a single individual to know these things.

The concept of utilitarianism emerges not only as an aspect of the social gospel, but is to be seen in the roots of liberation theology. Whatever action taken is designed to bring about a better state of affairs than offered by a world driven by competition and nationalism. The social gospel and liberation theology affirm that the aspiration of persons must be justice for all and prudence for the ''haves.'' In any case if people knew what to do to bring this about, they would have an ethical base.

Ethical Egoism

Another aspect of ethics that should be considered is egoism. This is an ethic of self-interest. We

185

need to understand all ethics has within it the characteristics of self-interest. Persons act in such a way that is good for them at least in the long run. We tend to be good because we *want* to be good people, we serve others because we *like* to serve others, and so on. But in this case the primary ethical question is concerned with what will bring about the greatest and most long-term benefits for me in a personal and narrow way. There is a tendency, of course, to see this as no ethics at all, or to call it pagan, or certainly anti-community, anti-American, or unchristian. All of these things might well be true but, at the same time, they are not. Egoism is a position that reflects deep feelings and assumptions about the nature of the universe. There is very little to say about it for it is fairly simple. It is best understood from its basic assumption: fulfilling individual desire is the proper end of human behavior.

The Ethics of Commitment

It is particularly true in the professions that persons who wish to accomplish something out of the ordinary—to rise above the heads of the average crowd—will be required to take risks. If such a role is one's own, then the question of success or failure may well rest with the intention rather than the outcome. The difficulty that most persons have with commitment is that it is not their own; rather, it is a trap in which they find that they are simply acting out the roles designed and assigned to them by others.

Again: Why Should I Be Moral?

We have acknowledged that this question is a

tough one. Also, it is often asked almost as an excuse when persons have already decided they will not be moral. For the average person stopped on the street, the answer to this question will be something like this: "If everyone is moral then it will be a better (meaning easier) world in which to live." This is probably true and in many ways a good point of view. But it is the answer to a different question. This answer addresses the question: "Why should *everyone else* be moral?" The question we are concerned with is why should *I*.

The most obvious and simple answer is this: "It is immoral not to be moral." But this does not help much.

At the beginning of this chapter I hinted at one reason why ethical behavior is so difficult. We will look further at it here. The most critical ethical decisions we make concern our attitude toward moral standards. It is not so much that we favor a particular stand and will not change. Nor is it that we decide to hold fast some kind of behavior. Rather, the difficulty lies in our willingness to allow our lives to be shaped by consideration of ethical choices.

The keystone to a child's ethics lies in the act of obedience. The conflict between what we have been told to do, and in doing what we please—is the point at which we face maturity. At this point children (regardless of age) can make one of several choices. They can choose to remain obedient, they can reject the standards of the significant others in their lives, they can conform only to avoid the difficulties that will follow violation, or they can take a personal look at it all, see what is involved, understand what needs to be decided, and then decide. At this last point they have espoused the criteria of maturity.

When arriving at such a point in ethical considerations, as in most events with human decisions, what people are looking for is a reason to be moral. In many cases they may well have arrived at the motive but are still held in check by the seriously asked question: "Why should I let the general values of the society in which I live override the personal self-interest that I can identify?" The answer is often one of moral maturity. And while there are many traditional answers as to what to do, the reasons for such a decision arise from that maturity.

Morality is not something you arrive at. Nor, I think, is it a stage. Rather, it is a process which at some point or other we might identify as mature. It assumes some responsibility not only to morality but to the person involved. The essence of such a maturity appears to lie in shaping one's being in a consistent fashion around commitment to fundamental human purposes. I know that is a mouthful, but I am trying to suggest that a maturity of ethical response has touches of consistency, commitment, human potential, relationships, and self-determination. Such an endeavor would be aware of and responsive to the limitations imposed by individuals, environments, beliefs, traditions, and social and interpersonal expectations. But the ethical response is not fixed by these. By the same token, freedom is expanded and growth determined by the knowledge of what affects human thinking and decision-making.

Morality presented in the terms of codes and rules will never serve as a panacea; rather, it will provide unity and solidarity in a life confronted with disagreements. It seems we have two choices. Persons can give their best to thinking rationally about how best to use the freedom they have. Or, persons give in to doing whatever they please, blowing like a leaf on the wind of every indecision or unaccompanied storm.

Let's Try Some Answers

Paying off on a promise made earlier, let me try and establish a short list of reasons for being moral. From the vast literature available these seem to be most acknowledged. Accept their limitations and see them as suggestions not as rules or duties.

1. The classical answer is that we would not be happy if we were not moral. This point of view reflects Plato's idea that persons are so created or designed that they seek a sense of morality. This morality, if violated, prevents them from being happy. Because all persons seem to have as their goal some degree of happiness (be it pleasure or salvation, it is still happiness) then the answer to the question is that we are moral in order to be happy. Or, at least, it keeps us from being unhappy.

2. Thomas Hobbes suggests in the *Leviathan* that persons are basically concerned with finding what he calls "the commodious life." He apparently means that humans seek to live a life which is peaceful, secure, and free not only from fear but from the "tooth and nail" strife of daily activity. We seek a life in which others will not take their victories from our limited resources: Life "will not rain on our parade." Because most of us are neither the strongest nor the smartest, we seek instead to find justice. The assumption being, then, that persons will forego particular interests in favor of gen-

eral interests. While they want to dispose of anyone who gets in their way, it is understood they could have no peace in a world if this were to happen. Thus, they are moral for their own best interests.

3. God tells us to be moral. This begs the issue a little because belief in God predetermines the disposition to be moral. However, to answer the question of *why*, a traditional answer has been because it is the command of God. We are determined to obey divine command, and that is moral.

4. Others say we are naturally good. Having been created good creatures—that is, persons with the natural tendency to do what we would consider to be good—then we are unnatural when we are not good. Given the possibility, a person will do the very best she or he can to act naturally. People do not seek to be unnatural. Thus we can say that persons are moral because it is their nature. While there is a good deal of evidence to the contrary (the assumption persons are basically good is questionable) this view acknowledges that moral behavior is just doing what comes naturally. To be immoral is to reflect a violation of your own nature—usually caused by some external force—about which you are not necessarily responsible.[5]

Quiz
1. What do we mean when we say "the *art* of ethics"?
2. Consider what the difference is (to you) between a motive that is to sanction, and a motive that is to conform.
3. Consider just how egotistical we are; thinking, for example, about how even loving someone is done for ourselves. Isn't the popular phrase "I

can't live without you''?

4. Try and list five *reasons* for being moral. Then list five *feelings* about why to be moral.

End Notes

1. F. H. Bradley, *Ethical Studies*, (Indianapolis: Bobbs-Merrill Library of Liberal Arts, 1951), 8.
2. P. H. Nowell-Smith, *Ethics* (Middlesex: Penguin Books, 1954), 226–231.
3. Nowell-Smith, 229.
4. Darrell Reeck, *Ethics for the Professions*, (Minneapolis: Augsburg Publishing House, 1982), 46.
5. Kai Nielsen, ''Why Should I Be Moral'' as quoted in William Frankena and John Granrose, *Introductory Readings in Ethics* (New Jersey: Prentice-Hall, Inc., 1974), 473–475.

A CASE IN POINT . . . A LITTLE LARCENY

We are told that dishonest workers cost the average company $1.50 per worker per day. While this figure depends a great deal on who is telling the story, the assumption is the same. Persons steal (borrow, lift, use, take, forget) from the persons for whom they work. This trait is so widespread and so acknowledged that companies actually make accounting entries charging the cost average to their employees' benefit plans. And, what is worse, no employee or employee representative has seen fit to challenge it.

Consider the following:

1. Do you steal from your employer or some institution with whom you work or associate? Why?

2. Do you consider that taking things from the office (stamps, paper clips, etc.) are such small crimes that they are not worth the concern? What would you consider a larger crime? How would you make the distinction?

191

3. How is this different from shoplifting? Is it different?
4. How do you respond to the idea that ''enforcing honesty is too costly''?

CHAPTER 11

A BRIEF HISTORY OF ETHICS

Anyone who doesn't know ethics is a sap. . . .
—Norman Gash

Questions of right and wrong have been around since the first cave creature questioned the appropriateness of stealing his neighbor's ox. Since that time, simple and complex responses have been proposed, systems have been developed, and principles expanded by every generation. In ethics the distinctions between periods of history is more clearly identified by the particular kinds of questions the ethical theory is addressing than they are by dates. It is possible to see the questions and answers of ethics relate historically to the contemporary economic, social, and theological questions being offered. "One advantage of learning about the history of ethics is that it frees us from a narrow concentration on the problems which seem important to our own times and gives us a wider perspective on the questions which have seemed important to other ages and cultures."[1] A brief history of that development is in order.

Pre-Socrates

One of the first accounts of ethical concern available to researchers is *The Book of the Dead* from 3500 B.C. One chapter in this collection of metaphysical ideas deals with the destiny of human beings. It supplies an early principle concerning their behavior. One's destiny, it asserts, is directly dependent on his or her conduct in this life. It recognizes that the question "What shall I do?" has applications to both the social world of our everyday behavior and to the ultimate world of our eternity. There is little in the book to describe what one should do, or how one is to know what to do. But the work obviously assumes individuals have control over their destinies and suggests that they are personally responsible for their actions.

In 1400 B.C. a man named Amenomope described what was probably "practical ethics" for his time. In the *Wisdom of Amenomope* he proclaims the necessity that persons refrain from robbing the poor and from failing to come to the aid of the old and the broken. He warns against taking upon one's self the essence of evil just because evil is being done. This view is based on a sense of moderation that was reflective of his time. In his work, however, he does not suggest why it is so or how the information about human behavior is established.

The classical Greek period reflects basic changes in the way persons looked at the world. This period expressed the beginning of some serious concern about how that world—or the larger universe in which it existed—could communicate with them. The Greeks displayed an increasing use of their minds as tools for understanding. They acknowledged an intellectual development in which persons are seen primarily as intellectual rather than emotional, where they pursue the philosophical rather than the religious, and where their lives and their thinking reflect moderation rather than extremes.

194

The Greeks seemed primarily concerned with living the good life. In general what they considered the good life was not so different from what most persons today see as the good life—that is, a life of happiness. But keep in mind these persons were more aware than we are that happiness is not necessarily pleasure. They saw happiness more in terms of peace of mind, moderation, balance, expectation without greed, and position without power.

Homer has ascribed to the gods all things that are a shame and a disgrace among mortals; stealings, and adulteries, and deceivings of one another.

—Xenophanes

Like today, every major intellectual action leads to a reaction. This was the case at the close of the fifth century B.C. when a period of criticism and deflation of metaphysical inquiry occurred. The exponents of this criticism and the emphasis on business as usual were a group known sarcastically as Sophists or wise ones. In return for teaching young persons the hard-nosed realities of business, the meaning of life, and the secrets of success (thus how to avoid the confusion and doubt of inquiry), they charged large fees which were freely paid.

This is not to suggest the Sophists reflected no moral principles, for in fact they did. But in the main they provided answers designed to prevent the need to seriously question one's behavior. Whether their answers were valid or designed to aid the business is yet another question. The primary

195

principle was "to be good is to be successful." For a man like Protagoras, moral behavior was teachable just like grammar. It is important to remember, however, that because all persons have different ambitions the moral codes will be different for each of them. Success meant basically what it means now: income, position, pride, political power, and pleasure.

Man is the measure of all things.
                                        —*Protagoras*

The Philosopher Kings

Socrates, the fifth century B.C. moralist, sought conceptions which were common or universal to all persons and positions. If people really admired the successful, if success in one's chosen field was the one thing that all persons could admire, it would seem there would be admiration for a successful tyrant, the successful murderer, or even the successful warrior when there is no war. This is not the case. Such persons do not even seem to find happiness. Perhaps, because there is no end to their need for more success, present success will not vanquish the desire. Socrates saw as more important the need to know *oneself* and to understand what it is that we want, to match it against what others want, and to find therein the universals that identify human behavior.[2]

His own inquiry leaves little room for doubt that he found virtue as the natural endowment of persons. If persons could only be brought to see virtue they would naturally follow it. Law and order are
196

part of these universal notions which are available in person's minds and which are of divine origin. They are memories of the soul's acknowledgment before individual birth. With help their memories can emerge from every human soul to lead and direct their behavior.

Virtue is knowledge.

—Socrates

In a series of essays, the philosopher Plato represented human beings as owners of souls which desire something they do not yet possess; they are incomplete. As rational persons they seek for—in fact are haunted by—the need for the ideal beauty, the ideal wisdom, the ideal ethic. Possessing the need and the ability to recognize these ideals once established, Plato's ethic reflects the fact that the *idea* is the true homeland for the human soul. Therefore, it is in the universal idea, the universal behavior, and the universal understanding that we find our peace, completeness, success, and thus our freedom.

The final ethical questions are directed to the fulfillment of these ideals. Persons are required to bring emotions and desires under the control of the intellect and, therefore, to conform to the ideals of justice, mercy, honesty, and virtue.

Aristotle was a pupil of Plato's and an admirer of much of what he saw. But in the final analysis he was a materialist who saw life best displayed in action not in idea. As an activist he saw the good life

197

as a life of accomplishment: doing things which were suggested by good principles. Aristotle was able to make the concept of moderation that was forever within the Greek structure into a principle—the doctrine of the golden mean. It was a balance between extremes, a line of departure that incorporated both of the extremes but did not take upon itself the self-destructive nature of the extreme.[3]

Just as courage is a proper balance between rashness and foolhardy involvement on the one hand and cowardice and irrational fear on the other, so does wisdom draw its balance between intellect and emotion. Extreme acts like murder, theft, and adultery are already excesses and, therefore, cannot exist in moderation. Persons, Aristotle determined, are drawn toward the highest good—the human end. The end includes a person's social as well as individual character. The end of a person is happiness—a personal *summum bonum*—attained by this rule of reason. Officially called *eudaemonism* (Greek meaning happiness), it is expressed or illustrated in friendship which serves the best interests of both the individual and the society. Aristotle stressed the good life as one in which power came to persons in the fullest and most harmonious balance.

Men love what is good for themselves; for the good man in becoming a friend becomes a good to his friend. Each then loves what is good for himself.

—Aristotle

Later, the charm of Epicurus' life and his appealingly liberal views on ethics and politics gave him an important following, particularly because his philosophy was one of salvation. He provided a philosophical ethic based on reasons which replaced the morality of descending religious convictions. His answer was simple. Behave, speak, think in the way that makes you the happiest. And what is happiness? It is physical pleasure. Called *hedonism* (Greek for pleasure) it stresses the best life embodying the maximum of pleasure. The attainment of this might well mean that one will incur pain to accomplish this purpose. That is probably okay. The human mind allows us to use intelligence and reason in such a way as to maximize the pleasure and diminish the pain, and this should be done. He went so far as to recognize that what is identified as pleasure may be nothing more than the ultimate absence of pain, realizing that we have to wait for positive pleasure and that we will only find it on occasion.

Happiness is a matter of the greatest amount of pleasure in the long run.

—Epicurus

Being fairly assured that human beings carry within them the price of their own happiness, Epicurus asserted that the purpose of life is to be happy. This means "not in pain." All persons can be happy if they accept the undeniable with cheerfulness and joy. Courage to prevent the ever-presence of fear and temperance to prevent the extremes from overcoming us are the greatest tools that humans have in dealing with these goals.

Stoics

This particular group of philosophers, known by the name of the porch in Athens where they used to gather to talk (the *Stoa Poikile*), followed a rigorous system created by reason and based on the natural state of events.

Virtue on its own is enough for blessedness.
—Zeno

The Stoics expected persons to live consistently with reason and with nature. Every animal, they suggested, is born with the same instinctive affection for itself. Stoicism acts in accordance with this affection and the need to protect and promote one's self. In humans, unlike other animals, reason aids in determining the appropriate action. This action becomes more accurate and consistent as our experience increases and allows us to control the desires of the immediate in return for long-range, harmonious relationships with nature. It acknowledges the difference between natural desires (as with food and warmth) and unnatural desires (gourmet food and fancy clothes). The Stoics affirmed that the ultimate outcome for ethical persons is to have as few desires and wants as possible. They did not want to eliminate desire, just have as few as possible by filling the natural ones and abolishing the desire for the unnatural. It is a form of moderation.[4]

The Roman World

The Roman contribution to ethics was like so many of Rome's contributions: a marriage of tradition with pragmatism. Cicero in the first century was perhaps the best spokesman. He tried to be the means of unity between Greek culture and Roman civilization. He bought the idea that persons have innate and common convictions which are reflected in human dignity, freedom, and immortality. His ethics combined the stern sense of duty available through the Stoics with the abstract conception of ideal behavior suggested by Plato. He was, nevertheless, a Roman and reflected his culture in his desire for rules which were clear and void of abstractions. Limited to a belief in the probability of knowledge, he had to accept a probability of ethics as well. But he stressed fairness as the primary tool for human decisions about theology and ethics.

The impact of the Jewish and Christian religions on ethics is so significant as to be beyond analysis. The Jewish nation was founded on revelation and that is true of its ethics. Revelation, rather than reason or philosophical speculation, was the foundation of behavior and morality. Based on God, the revelator, the Jewish nation developed a code of behavior that turned out to be much harsher than before. The question for Christians was less legalistic but was also based on sets of behavior concepts. The Christian was perhaps less harsh but no less dogmatic. The primary question became, "How can I live right with God?"[5]

While the teaching of Jesus and the institutionalization of his ideas are not really an ethical theory, they are most definitely an evaluation of life-style. This ethic is based on the two principles of Jesus:

love and sacrifice. The former is not so unusual for it was taught by other religious leaders like Confucius and Buddha, it is the basic teaching of the Bhagavad Gita, and it is the key to the prophet Hosea and Rabbi Hillel. Sacrifice was also a key to the teachings of religious leaders and no list of supporters could be complete. What was so central and unique in Jesus was the radical nature of his love: to love one's enemies and to connect this love directly to a loving God.[6]

The Judeo-Christian expression brought forward the idea of the family of all persons under the supreme parental leadership of God. Facing the growth of nationalism, this worked to show that persons had worth in the sight of God and thus should be treated with worth among persons. If weak, persons must be helped. If sinners, they must be saved. If vindictive, they must be converted. Hatred against one's fellow persons is evil and against the love of God. This love of God is to be reflected in one's neighbors and thus the essence of morality becomes associated with the treatment of others and is found more and more in community. One of the basic differences between this tradition and the twentieth century is this emphasis on community.

The Jewish ethic emphasizes a detailed response and obedience to the Mosaic law. It is practiced both ethically and ceremonially. That is, it is the result of being obedient to the specific details of the law as well as celebrating the abstractive nature of the law. It involves keeping the commandments, observing dietary and ceremonial laws, and in the continuing customs and traditions based on the study of the Torah.[7]

Catholic and Response

Through the long history of the church and its inherent characteristic of change through leaders and spokesmen, Catholicism has taken many stands. In the main, however, it has been based on an emphasis on good works. It is a religion directed toward the training of our wills into proper and expected submission to the will of God. Of course, it does not rely only on good works, for good works without faith and the help of God are basically without worth. However, the expression of this faith and the emphasis of God's continued involvement is to be found in these works. Associated with this is the practice of obedience, confession, the training of the will, and the works of devotion and charity.

The diversity of the Protestant movement makes it harder to generalize than about Catholicism. But in the main, Protestantism has emphasized the importance of faith, the expectations of grace, and the experience of conversion to God. Good works are the natural and expected results of faith in God and are a sign of conversion. It is the acceptance of God through Jesus Christ that is the basis of the ethic and the behavior through which one is measured.

Of course, ethical systems without God were budding in this period as well. Humanism—an ethical system without external source—was developing. The idea of laws without lawgivers was of increasing importance. This arose after the Reformation partly because of a weakened Christianity and partly due to a more generalized skepticism about the role of religion. Religion had not produced the effects it sought, and this was an age beginning to test a product by its conclusions.

The British Tradition

Based on an appeal to experience rather than reason or inherent concepts, the British tradition sought an ethics of relationships that existed between persons rather than one which existed between persons and their God.

The sixteenth-century English gentleman, Thomas Hobbes, was the spokesman for a good portion of the ethical base that was emerging. Ethics deals with the mental notions—the processes—of the body and reflects both the desires and the repulsions. Men and women naturally desire power like they desire other things, and it is the intellectual control of such power—and eventually other things—that gives persons their chance. Hobbes felt that we should treat other persons in such a way as to protect ourselves from them and to bring them into cooperation with our particular plan. People by nature are less than trustworthy. But they are bright and they will understand the need to act together for their own best interests. Persons are equal in their rights and wills and are common in their desires. Compromise is the only way out of the chaos which would result if all had their way. The first law of nature is that persons will deliberately seek peace. The second law of nature is that humans are willing to place controls on the unbridled exercise of their own rights in order to secure freedom from the unbridled expectations of others. All human interests are best served in an organized society in which common experience can be used to prevent war, social unrest, and individual defeats. Richard Purtill has suggested that for Hobbes ethics has turned out to be sort of social engineering.

> *The mutual transferring of rights is that which men call contracts.*
>
> *—Hobbes*

Dave Hume, an eighteenth-century Scottish philosopher, expressed belief that morality is an artificial state for persons. There is, he asserted, no absolute or moral imperative imposed on humans. He held the position, unlike Plato, that our intellect has no desires and thus is the best source of control over our emotions and appetites. The intellect has only the intention of meeting the goals established by our desires. Moral concepts are sentiments and thus our good and our bad reflect only feelings—pleasure and discontent—gained from behavior. Any system we construct will be based on these needs not on any instinctive affection for humans.

The treatment of humans, then, can be measured by realizing the degree to which they help fulfill our own passions, understanding that these passions include altruistic and benevolent ones. Because moral action is not determined by reason, it must be discerned by "moral sense"—a peculiar capacity to feel—which places the rightness and wrongness of acts within us. This results in a "convention of agreement" so as to pursue one's intent among persons.[8]

Utilitarianism

Under the leadership of men like Jeremy Bentham and John Stuart Mill, the utilitarians found a system based on the greatest good for the greatest number over the greatest length of time. Based on a

205

communitarian concept and beginning with a moral sense of goodness (however they wished to define it), they tended to clash with both "common sense" and legalistic ethics.

There appear to be about as many kinds of utilitarianism as there are persons who espouse them, but for our purposes it is enough to identify the idea in its simplest form. Utilitarianism holds that an action is right (good) to the degree that the action brings about happiness for the largest number of persons within a defined community. Therefore, an act is bad (wrong) to the degree it decreases happiness or increases pain. Happiness in this view means without pain. Mill, along with most of his followers, believed and advocated freedom. Freedom of opinion is not so much a right to which pesons are entitled, however, as it is a discipline of which they stand in need and are usually disinclined to accept.

Immanuel Kant

This significant nineteenth-century gentleman is one of the most important philosophers of our time. He derived a moral theory based on his analysis of the means by which intellectual beings must guide their own conduct. Morality, he said, is primarily a matter of will itself, not the success of the will. It is to be judged not by its consequences but by its self-consistency. He recognized that it could not be based on description. There is plenty of evidence for understanding this position. Rather, Kant felt the need to base morality on principles about humans and their relationships to the cognizant nature of other created things. Such a situation must emphasize intentions rather than performance.[9] The universal principle as he understood it requires that we always deal with other persons as ends not as means to ends. Such a rule is self-imposed. If we act morally by this universal principle we are not only citizens of the world but are, by virtue of the universality of the law, "citizens of the Kingdom of ends" in which we are both the citizens and the rules. If we are obedient to the laws we have imposed, we can find no greater truth than to be good rulers by virtue of being good citizens. There is no compromise, no trade; nothing can be sold or moved about these rules. God, unable to will other than to do good, is also bound by these laws; thus the universal nature of God's obedience is added to the spontaneousness of our action.

Act so as to treat humanity, whether in thine own person or in that of any other, in every case as an end withal, never as a means only.
—I. Kant

Contemporary Ethical Theory

One of the characteristics of the contemporary world is the degree to which the ideas and traditions of past generations are still present and active. In addition to simply carrying on the understandings of previous centuries, however, the modern generation has been preoccupied with questions about the validity of moral action and/or the existence of ethical principles. After all, a civilization that finds itself more and more willing to do what previous civilizations would not even talk about cannot be overly concerned with perennial standards. Part of this whole questioning process, however, started before the "me" generation found its place. One such early anticipator was Frederick Nietzsche who had interpreted the idea of self-realization as basically egotistical.

In seeking the "Superman" humanity persons must first of all release themselves from the values by which they now live, especially the morality of the Jewish-Christian ethic. It is "the work of creatures too weak to face life as it is, too fearful of it to fight it, too feeble to enjoy it, and too spiritually flabby to work out their own salvation from its terrors and its dangers"[10] Christian ethics is not the work of Christ, Nietzsche points out to us, for Christ was strong, lived without rancor and existed with the serenity that emerges out of power. His was a mystical awareness of being at home. Thus, as Christ found his own being in his sense of oneness with the whole universe, humans will transcend human good and human evil and find their morality in their oneness with the universe. They will become whole in identifying themselves with the whole.

It was Frederick Hegel who identified self-realization on the individuals' behalf as part of developing self-realization for the whole human race. Hegel's principles are expressed in terms of contracts. In contracts, individuals publicly limit themselves by their realization—and then their agreement—and they will refrain from certain action in order to maintain a society in which these actions do not occur. There are no principles here as they have been traditionally defined, only an agreement; there is no truth here, only a signed document. The private will shall welcome the restraints of the public will. Only in such restraints can the
208

private will function. But we must remember it is *will* not truth.

Another philosopher who has been partially responsible for more current trends is R. M. Hare. His questions are about the properties—the characteristics—of ethics. He says that if two basketballs are alike in essence and are only different in that one of them is white and the other black, it would seem reasonable to say that if two ideas existed— one being different only in that it was bad and the other was good—that there was no more difference in the essence of the idea than in the essence of the basketballs. Good and bad, like white and black, are secondary or consequential characteristics not inherent like simple properties. That is to say, an idea is never good or bad (nor is anything), only an idea; we attach good and bad to it.

This tends to lead to a kind of subjectivism which suggests that ethical behavior—thus morality—is dependent on the individual judgment of the persons involved. It is neither based on the external world (no matter how relative that may be) nor on any sort of universal concept. Ethics is a matter of individual decision. It is based on the assumption that whatever an individual person decides to do is right (for that person) under every circumstance. In a strict sense this is not really ethics because it is the nature of ethics to be involved in identifying moral truth and principles of conduct. And this does not. But it is the basis for a lot of ethical reasoning and rationalization.

Situation Ethics

Often this is seen as being subjective or relativistic, and in some forms it is. But more than that, of course, it is an ethic of love which—because it places love as the determination factor—appears to be relativistic and subjective. This morality rejects the concept of legalism (thus formalism) and takes the position that true love is all that ultimately matters. The difficulty is that most of us do not know how to act out of love. St. Augustine was reported to have said "Love God and then do what you will,"[11] but such a statement assumes that if you love God well you will only will to do what is godly. Situation ethics is more likely to say that if you love well and act out of love, then you will do that which is loving. It may cause other harm, it may not be best for society, but it will not hurt the persons whom you love.

Universalizability and Contextualism

The first is a theory which suggests that moral judgments may well be individual. It accepts that they may also be particular to the time and place they are made. But they always imply a universal judgment. This is based on an idea presented by R. M. Hare and reflective of the work of Immanuel Kant. It holds that while we are dealing with a particular problem, the problem contains universal implications that prevent it from being either arbitrary or contextual. When we say that "Joe should not kill" we mean that "No one should kill and Joe is no exception." It suggests the attempt to make a moral argument rather than a moral description: "Joe should not kill" rather than "Joe will not kill."

The second view—contextualism—stands in opposition to any sort of universal law. It says that the relevant criteria for working out significant ethical

210

decisions lie within the "context of a given situation. Thus contextualism would hold that every problem is unique (not just relative to a culture as relativists say) and thus every ethical decision is unique. All the factors to be weighed in arriving at the decision lie in the situation. These decisions, like the evidence for them, are concrete and fundamental. If you are willing the well-being of another (assuming your own well being), then whatever you do will be determined by the situation you are in.

Existentialism

We have discussed existentialism in some detail in the context of this work. Primarily this ethical position (or lack of position) has pushed individualism to the ultimate extreme. Generally existentialism is opposed to both rational and empirical points of view because both seem to deal with the universe as if it were determined in a prior fashion. Existentialism, however, turns to irrationalism to view the world. Human essence, like human behavior patterns, will emerge from the individual's own unfolding response to the world. It is not predictable, it is not a matter of principles, it is not predetermined. It is unique.

Relativism

Usually called "cultural relativism," this point of view states that ethical laws are not, in reality, law. This is true because there is no absolute nature to them. Perhaps suggested by Aristotle's "fire burns both in Hellas and in Persia: but men's ideas of right and wrong vary from place to place."[12] Certainly they would hold that there is no universal good or bad, right or wrong. Rather, laws are rules of behavior established by the wishes and desires of the community that develops them. What is right are the behavior guidelines that provide the outcome the society wishes to provide.

It is hard to tell just how popular—and in the long run how important—the trends of our day really are. There is a lot of evidence, however, that persons are more and more willing to turn to what has been defined as the "Zany Myths" for answers. Having found their own myths faulty, they seek some new or resurrected story to explain their world and to give meaning to their questions. Among these myths are the reemergence of astrology and zodiacal signtelling, publications of things like Shirley MacLaine's *Out on a Limb* or the immensely popular *Ramtha,* the latter being the advice of a person who is reported to be 30,000 years old. Of the same vintage are lotteries with their instant riches, television game shows such as "The Price Is Right," and national interest (including my own) in cartoon strips like "Snoopy" and "The Far Side," as well as the huge sales of *The Hug Therapy Book.*

These are ethics of universalism but they name no source. They represent a deep need to fill some of the gaps that exist in value orientation. It is beyond the scope of this book to try and determine where they come from, why persons have so willingly accepted and followed such strange ethical myths, or build life-systems on the audio tapes of a 30,000-year-old medium. It remains to be seen if any of these ethics will survive, or if this is but another in a long history of fads which work their way in and around more traditional ethical responses.

Quiz

Place the letter which identifies the description in the space provided.

_____ 1. "To be good is to be successful."

_____ 2. "Know oneself."

_____ 3. "Seek moderation in all things."

_____ 4. Based on the Greek word for pleasure

_____ 5. "Virtue on its own is enough. . . ."

_____ 6. A radical principle of loving

_____ 7. Ethics is a contract.

_____ 8. "Love God and then do what you will."

A. Sophists
B. Aristotle
C. Zeno
D. Hedonism
E. Augustine

F. Hobbs
G. Socrates
H. Christian
I. Judaic

End Notes

1. Richard Purtill, *Thinking About Ethics* (New Jersey: Prentice-Hall, Inc., 1976), 134–135. As noted I am indebted to Purtill for form and order in this chapter.
2. Purtill, 132.
3. Purtill, 133.
4. Purtill, 133–134.
5. Purtill, 135.
6. See Brightman, *Moral Laws*, 19.
7. Purtill, 135.
8. Purtill, 137.
9. Purtill, 138.

10. McMurrin, Vol. II, 450.
11. Russell Shaw, *Choosing Well* (London: University of Notre Dame Press, 1982), 78–79.
12. "Nicomachean Ethics," Anthony Flew, *A Dictionary of Philosophy* (New York: St. Martin's Press, 1979), 281.

CHAPTER 12
CONCLUSIONS

The love of life at any and every level of experience is a religious impulse. To recognize this may be the beginning of wisdom and a reasonable approach to an understanding of the voice within.

—Marcus Bach

According to legend Gyges was a shepherd for the kingdom of Lydia. He found a magical ring that gave him the power to be invisible. In this state he could do exactly as he wished. And, in time, he seduced the Queen and killed the King, then placed himself on the throne of Lydia for forty years. His was a great ethical dilemma for he could take what he wanted and never be seen; he could cheat and murder without being caught. He was able to live his life without being held accountable for any of his actions. As he considered his life, Gyges was to wonder if his previous behavior had been based on a belief in some form of inherent goodness or was it in fact just dependent on his fear of being caught. That is a vital question for most of us.

If there is no social consequence to one's actions (crimes), is there punishment? If there is no social punishment for our actions, do the actions themselves punish us in some way? Is punishment a justification for an action or a deterrent? Is there—or should there be—any connection between unethical behavior and punishment? When asking these questions as individuals it is sometimes helpful to consider what your behavior would be like if you were immune from all punishment.

As I write this Colonel Oliver North, U.S. Marine Corps, once a trusted employee of the National Security Council and an officer in a proud service, is being considered for immunity from prosecution for any crimes he may have committed. The hope is that if granted immunity he will identify others who were also guilty. What does such action say to him as well as to the other citizens when he is encouraged to avoid responsibility for his violations of social law and sacred trust? In many respects Colonel North and others in government and big business are like Gyges. They have seen themselves as being able to act without anyone knowing it. They feel they have been made invisible by power or the overwhelming structure of government. What would you do? Would you feel free to do as you please, to do what you felt like at the moment? Or would you be inclined to act in the same manner as always, looking to the same values? Some years ago John Oman addressed this question.[1]

There is only one right way of asking men to believe, which is to put before them what they ought to believe because it is true; and there is only one right way of persuading, which is to present what is true in such a way that nothing will prevent it from being seen except the desire to abide in darkness; and there is only one further way of helping them, which is to point out what they are cherishing that is opposed to faith.

As Christians we recognize our need to be representatives of Christ in our world. Our purpose is to heal the wounded and broken world in which we live. We recognize with V. A. Demant that humans cannot choose between God and mammon until they have learned to distinguish the difference "that (distinction) it is religion's responsibility to

216

make plain." It is not sufficient for the church to encourage ethical behavior. The church must aid persons in the identification of the ethical questions and strengthen them in their moral resolve. But most of all, the church must help in arriving at ethical conclusions.

At some point we must join with William Coffin to say explicitly, "There is no way that Christianity can be spiritually redemptive without being socially responsible. A Christian cannot have a personal conversion experience without experiencing at the same time a change in social attitude. God is always trying to make humanity more human."[2] Remember, Coffin says, "every time we lift our eyes to heaven and cry out, 'Lord...how long shall the wicked triumph? How long shall they utter and speak hard things' at that very moment you can be sure God is putting precisely the same question to us. So our calling is simply to help God protect, affirm, and dignify life—more and more of it."[3] We must lay the haunting fears of risk aside and be involved in participation. To the question "Moses, Moses, where are you" came the only reply possible. "Here I am." Up until that time Moses had been playing a spectator's role. Now he became part of the solution.

If the church is to serve any role for its member communities, then the church must take responsibility to provide aids and directions, to develop insights, and to serve in identifying what best serves God's interests in the world. This is not a suggestion that the church should provide a set of answers. History has shown the problems with that. Rather, it encourages understanding and aids in the establishment of principles. For the church can and

217

must be involved in identifying such principles. It is important, then, that the church be involved in dialogue with and between ethical persons. It must help in expressing the best of all arguments, and be in the business of learning from the differences that exist among persons of good will.

The good that arises from the consideration of conflicting values does not emerge from the condemnation of the destruction of others. But, as Dorothy L. Sayers has so well demonstrated, the good that emerges does so from the new values sustained by the tension of the two. We do not look at old ideas, or different cultures, in order to impose one upon the other. But rather to build anew, to create anew, to emerge from what was not totally acceptable into something meaningful: something that was not there before, and which arises from our own efforts as well as our own passions.[4]

When a generation begins the process of defining its own moral concerns, it is immediately confronted with the forms and ideas which the previous generation took to heart. From these the process of ethical definition takes on two forms: reception and liberation. The reception is acknowledging what the previous generation has accomplished and what effect it has had on their own lives. Liberation is from the institutionalization of previous ideas. Liberation from the ''oughtness'' which allows them to think and act freely. Free so that the creative genius inherent in the new generation can be released and flow into areas as yet undiscovered or unexplained.[5]

History shows us that every generation feels its problems are the most significant. But it would be hard to find a time when the relationship between spirituality and morality in the church has been more strained. The church's need for an expression of its own vulnerability has led to pronouncements of doubt. This is reflective of the individual search for identity and acceptance which has made persons poor citizens of the church community. The desperate human needs are, in the main, as yet unmet. The ability of the church to apply the values and the hopes of the ancient gospel to the complex issues of modern, moral life is desperately lacking. Some say the gospel has no meaning today. Others contend civilization has become so corrupt it cannot hear universal truths. The crisis has often produced efforts to manipulate truth, to mold the truth to speak to whatever we wish to have done. But this is morally dangerous and is more—rather than less— dangerous when it is done for pious reasons. We must be very careful that the church community speaks only as it has seriously and faithfully understood.

Having a Position

At the same time as we recognize the care with which we approach ethical pronouncements, we must not forget that as a people we have convictions which represent ethical principles. Members of the RLDS Church have taken some considerable heart from the acceptance of pluralism. But a word of caution. Pluralism does not mean we have no convictions, no positions, and that all points of view are equally as acceptable. That is more aptly labeled "wishy-washy." Pluralism means that the church is open enough to have within it a variety of strongly held and well-supported positions which differ. While we are probably wise not to claim to have *the*

219

answers and, in some cases, have no inclination to make any pronouncement at all, it is nevertheless, true that our religious convictions support ethical principles. It would seem significant that we be aware of these principles and encourage the community to consider them carefully in the development of its own ethical positions.

Hopefully we will be alert to the fact that such principles are often tied to national or sociological debts or attached too tightly to cultural needs. We will need to be aware of the ever-present conflict between individual and institutional needs. But we feel free to express our belief in Christian love, and thus should be just as free to suggest other universal understandings that affect our behavior. This can be done without superiority of position or attacks on other positions.

Pascal is quoted as saying "the most insidious thing about error is that it, as a rule, deals with something in itself true, but which is untrue because it excludes something equally true."[6] I find this a very important aspect of human behavior. It is a significant part of developing an individual— and eventually an institutional—view of ethics. I am not willing to say that the ethical understandings of this generation are necessarily wrong or that persons have cast all ethics aside in their pursuit of freedom. My problem with this generation's principles is that they have not reaped the rewards anticipated. I would be more inclined to accept a world free of all values (other than the value of freedom) if we were getting what it was that we expected from this stand. The most difficult aspect of our spiral toward freedom without measure is that it is not only spiritually defeating, it does not work.

220

I do not find any evidence that people are any more free today (spiritually, psychologically, morally) than they were fifty years ago.

Many persons still profess to be religious. This is true, just as they profess to have appreciation for philosophy, literature, and art. We must acknowledge that they believe this is true. But to a large degree the values they profess have been driven out of their daily lives. They have become special values. Someone has called them "Sunday Values." They are carefully identified and located in places where they can be found, even appreciated, but rarely used. It is a fact of our lives that religion has been relegated to something we do at an appointed time and place. It is something we work *at* not in. We practice religion; we do not profess it.

It is also true, I believe, that ethical understandings have taken the same path. That persons consider the study of ethics to be just that, a study. Under current circumstances persons are concerned about ethics but do not profess them. They do not see any relationship between the principles they would like to espouse and the behavior they feel it is necessary to follow. "This is business, after all, and we cannot. . . ." And then follows a long line of things that we would "like" to do but "cannot" do because they are costly, inconvenient, precedent setting, or an interference with one's individual agenda of success.

Crane Brinton has used the word *conduct* to suggest what persons actually do. He has used the word *ethics* to identify the basic principles behind their actions. Thus he has left the word *morals* to sum up the total human situation in which action, evaluation of action, and judgment take place. Morality,

221

as he sees it, is both the "is" and the "ought" of human existence and includes an awareness of the past, the present, and the future.[7] It is both what is, and what ought to be, now, and in the future.

William Coffin has identified what he thinks is the key to the "problem of the Christian Church in America today: most of us fear the cure more than the illness. Most of us prefer the plausible lie that we cannot be cured to the fantastic truth that we can be. And there is a reason: if it's hell to be guilty, it's certainly scarier to be responsible."[8]

Doing and Believing:

Philosophers, particularly those who teach introduction to philosophy courses, often hear the charge: "It doesn't matter what you think, only what you do." For our own sakes, and the sake of those with whom we share community, it is important not to minimize the primary relationship that exists between what we think and what we do. Continued and unresolved control on the outer expression, as well as limitations imposed by persons on their inward expression, all seem to come back to haunt us. In the long run persons are strongly motivated to resolve the "cognitive dissonance" that emerges when they are torn between what they believe and what they do—what we tend to call "mixed emotions." Eventually every effort will be made by the rational person to solve the inconsistency between what they personally and privately believe and what they personally and publicly say. Richard Crutchfield warns us that if "persons cannot say what they really believe they may end up believing what they say."

It is not difficult for us to recognize in others con-
222

flicts between what they say and what they do: the person who preaches honesty while stealing. When this circumstance becomes particularly glaring and difficult, we call it hypocrisy. The hypocrite who is aware that he or she is doing one thing and saying or espousing another is more rare than you might at first imagine. It is more and more evident that persons who appear to be hypocrites are more likely involved in what psychologists call "denial" or "defense." We are often able to keep conflicts of reality totally out of our minds. We do not see them. Such persons may not be unethical even though they appear to be acting in a manner that would seem to be unethical. This ability to divorce the evil that we do from the ideals that we hold seems to be widespread and is, some would say, the basis of modern justice.

Another response by those for whom doing and being seems to be confused, is to claim indifference. How many times have you heard someone say, "It does not matter what a person believes"? What we often think of as indifference or as broad-mindedness is little more than a kind of moral and intellectual irresponsibility. In our participation in the world it seems as irresponsible to suggest indifference to God, to persons, or to moral responsibility as to suggest that one is indifferent to electricity and to germs. "Indifferentism, moreover, is a travesty on freedom; for no man is free to believe what he pleases."[9]

Gurus and Enlightenment

If you ask a six year old "What is the meaning of life?" you should be ready for about anything. The child may answer: "To grow up" or "To be happy."

We accept that for what it is, the not overly considered view of a young and still immature mind. This, of course, does not mean that they are wrong.

When we climb to the top of the craggiest mountain of the Tibetian ranges seeking the words and advice of a great guru, we might well discover that he, too, gives us the answer, "To grow up" or "To be happy." This answer is the same but we are more likely to consider the guru's answer to be true.

But with all due respect to gurus—and I have respect—the chances are that this answer is no more "philosophical" than the first. Gurus are mystic or secular leaders who have arrived at some sort of insight or enlightenment as a result of their vast ponderings. The image of a guru sitting on the top of a mountain contemplating his or her navel is, of course, an improper image. For gurus—by definition—have already arrived at their level of spiritual truth or maturity. And rather than thinking about it they are participating in it.

For us, gurus operate in a nonphilosophical manner as well. For the gurus offer serenity, peace of mind, and answers to all questions. They are generally unaffected in their life-styles by the questions of the mind. They arrive, as did Siddhartha after years of searching, at the "truth" by which they will live. They no longer need to question or consider. Rather, they provide what Woodhouse has called "psychological generalizations" which are addressed to the psyche rather than to reason. Again we are not talking about them being wrong— like the child, they could be right on target. They are professors of a cause or a case rather than investigators of systems and answers.

Philosophers, you will remember from your readings, are not concerned about making ethical pronouncements. Instead, they are involved in looking at the continuous unfolding of the principles they have begun to identify and isolate. They are also concerned with presenting these in such a way that persons' ethical involvement continues to represent the best understanding we have. In the long run the child, the guru, and the philosopher will be making an analysis of their best thinking at that point in time. However, the philosopher, like the child, is still looking for that illusive *justified true belief.*

In this frame of reference, I am inclined to suggest that the immediate culmination of my own philosophical (ethical) ponderings is a sort of post-rational position. Not post-rational in the sense something is being substituted for reason. It is rather a suggestion that though the foundations of my beliefs are rational and analytical, much of what is important to and about human beings must be gleaned by pushing beyond that which is available only in the rational. Let me say again, I am not suggesting we must not reason to the best of our ability. Only that once reasoning has been done, there is much to be gained by moving beyond thought into a world in which feelings and understandings emerge.

This means that what becomes important in *my* inquiry is not limited by the confines of logical maneuvering. It also means I am unwilling to accept the lack of a coherent world view as a limitation. I do not need to have an explanation for everything I see or feel. Somehow when we are through putting the picture puzzle of life together, we always have unexplained pieces left over. Pieces which fit, and could be substituted, where we have already placed pieces. And, were we to exchange them, the picture would change. The pressure to analyze every definition, to trace every word to its ultimate degree of meaning, and to count and articulate every qualitative character of a sentence, goes beyond what I think philosophy is about. Or perhaps I should say it fails to go far enough into what philosophy is about.

I would suggest the importance of philosophical inquiry is to better understand what it means to be human. My ponderings are concerned with the human situation and the effort to find relevance in life rather than precision in description. I acknowledge the great need to move beyond a world where we are inclined to give away our freedom, compartmentalize our thinking, justify our irrelevance, and utilize our mediocrity. We have replaced our participation with an increasing need to have, to possess, and to acknowledge personhood in terms of doing.

The proper role of philosophy is to make persons more sensitive to the conditions which affect them, to bring persons into a sense of understanding about their world conditions, and to make it possible for them to appreciate and share in the wholeness we see represented in the best of things. To me, the measure of philosophy is the difference it makes in persons' lives.

Ethical Base

I am not content to leave you here, hopefully full of information and anxious to be about the business of identifying ethical principles. I am inclined to offer some ideas for consideration. I have numbered these ethical comments for sake of clarity not

226

because of some hierarchy. You are urged to remember these are my points of view. I ask you only to look at them within the context of this work. Then in the best manner you can, formulate your own conclusion. Write your own last chapter.

1. The church is not an exclusive community of persons who have the same point of view or necessarily the same behavioral standards. It is a community of persons made up of those who recognize the claim of Jesus Christ on their lives and who have at least some faith in him as the supreme love giver. In most cases this faith will be weak and faltering. Likewise, we will most likely be inconsistent and often sinful. It is by the mercy of God that we have rights in the community and by the mercy of the community that we find social meaning there. The church is meant for persons who need help. It is meant for sinners. Thus the church must be very careful about the exclusion of those that Christ has invited. While we hope for the best within the human community—as in God's community—we must remember we are limited and must make every effort to be loving, and accepting of persons rather than always evaluating the performance of others.[10]

2. The essential knowledge of history has been to aid people in the restoration of their own life narratives. Absorbed as we so often are in the concerns of the moment and enslaved by the pragmatic needs of today and tomorrow, we are more than ever in need of a sense of proportion. People need some appreciation for the vastness of time, for its duration, and for the lack of territorialness in that which is eternal. We are products not only of the Jewish and the Christian heritage—as well as the

heritage of our nations and our families—but of the Restoration and the Reorganization as well. Much of what we think of as right and wrong reflects that tradition. An awareness of this past, this tradition, is essential if we are to rise above either the judgments or the provocations of the movement. Whatever we may decide to do, we must not make that decision in a vacuum. Nor, it is important to remember, do others make their decisions in a vacuum. Knowledge of who and what we are is essential to our ethical decisions.

3. Certainly if we are able to see love as central to the Christian concept of human behavior, then we must also be willing to see humility as the primary corrective of that behavior. A Christian understanding of the degree of our own failures ought to be enough to control the human tendency to assume we are right. And while we may feel very right about what we believe, our experience needs to teach us of the horrible consequences of persons too quick to assume their beliefs are universal laws. The teachings of Christ transcended all human dimensions. Our acceptance of them should aid in avoiding the tendency to make an absolute of everything *we* think. The humility that comes from the awareness of our mistakes, of misunderstandings, and of our simple humanness must serve to keep us ever open to God's direction.[11]

Associated with this humility is the realization that there is little purpose, and not much accomplished, in asserting the correctness of our understanding unless we are willing to accept the obligations of that assessment. Norman Angell states it this way.

The price of the right to assert our view is a firm sense of the obligation to let others assert contrary views, and to listen to them; to make the first impulsive thought subject to the second more disciplined thought; to face the fact that the voice of the people (which is you and me) is usually the voice of Satan; that we are subject to pugnacities, passions, prejudices which it is our duty to see do not run away with us.[12]

4. Our generation has somehow managed to suggest that there is little or nothing we cannot know. Scientists (at least technocrats) have suggested to us that there is very little we cannot have. The fact that we do not know and do not have is explained by the lack of time or interest or money. Nothing else. Thus persons have been appeased in their ignorance by the promise of meaning and in their acquisitions by the accumulation of objects. We have been more than a little concerned with the lack of answers but are refreshed by the promise that answers exist.

Likewise, the constitutional right to "pursue happiness" has been translated by our generation into the right to *have* happiness, feeling somehow, that not to be happy is symbolic of a general failure to meet the standards of weight, size, car model, toothpaste, soft drink, or other marks of "happy" people. The promise of salvation given by churches has been translated into a kind of grace which requires no contribution. And, in the main, we do not take into consideration the hope of a godly response from the people.

There is a great deal we do not and cannot know. Much we must accept on faith. There are many things about which we shall simply have to make decisions without adequate proof. It is likewise true that we shall not always be happy in terms of our every desire being met, each hope realized. The

229

contentment that life offers is one of fulfillment, of completion. It lies in the having of dreams rather than the realization of them, in acknowledging our humanness and being happy—content—because of it.

We do not pursue loving relationships because power has become more appealing, more dependable. Betrayed ourselves, we find greater security in being the betrayer. Nicholas Machiavelli advised would-be rulers "it is significant to be loved, but more dependable to be feared." More modern philosophy states it this way: "Yea, though I walk through the valley of the shadow of death I shall fear no evil, for I am the meanest one in the valley." One way, we are told, to avoid being afraid of exploitation by the mugger in the park is to *be* the mugger in the park. I dare say that we would not buy this thesis but, of course, in a very real sense we have. For power has often replaced listening, replaced caring, and replaced human relations. It is the ever-increasing response of "I-IT" in which our excuses for treating others as objects rest in our assumption that if they do not control they are to be controlled.

We see this everywhere. We adopt it everywhere. The "power syndrome" assumes because we *can* control that we *must* control, and because such significance is given to the *must* it serves as an excuse for exploitation. This is true of the pastor who silences those in opposition, of the church school director who uses a person's commitment to foist off unacceptable levels of work, to the deacon who leaves persons standing in order to show them who is in charge. We see it in bosses who use their economic power in the workplace to demand personal favors. We see it in the exploitation of the weak, in the violation of the committed, in the mistreatment of the dedicated, and in the "favorite son" expectations of those who win because they like winning. It is seen as well in the arrogance of power which assumes that control means intelligence, that office suggests knowledge, and in the arrogance of "levels" of ministry or "rights" of service.

5. Explanation is not justification. I remember with great clarity the military explanation of this: "Edwards, there may be a reason for your behavior" the crusty old corporal would say "but there is no excuse." It is important to remember that to know *why* you do something is not a *just reason* for doing it. If your mother asks you why you ate the apple pie, your answer "I was hungry" is a statement of cause. But what she is really asking is "Why did you eat the piece of apple pie I saved for your Aunt Jane?" Then the answer is "I am inconsiderate." When you ask persons who seem to have accomplished the impossible why they did it, you may hear the familiar "because it was there." They are not talking about justification but rather about cause. Why we do something must be recognized as meaning both "What was the reason?" and "What events led up to this event?" In our relationship with others we often confuse an explanation with justified reasons for the action. More careful consideration should remind us that persons are not objects upon which we act, but others—other I's—with whom we must relate.

6. As I have suggested in another place, much of persons' inability to deal with behavior in the contemporary world rests in the insistence that life is a

problem to be solved. I am more inclined to think life is, instead, an adventure to be lived, a process to be participated in, a search in which to be involved. When we assume that our every activity is a problem, then what we are searching for is a way to solve it, to bring the activity or its consequences to a conclusion. On the other hand, when we see life as participation, we are aware of the need to grasp it, to become at one with it, and to share in the wholesomeness of the universe into which we have been created.

This wholesomeness involves us in a sense of awareness about ourselves and our world. It is about personal integrity. It means participating in a manner that does not violate the unity of ourselves or our relationships with the unity that is all of us.

a. Participation involves an awareness of the situation of others so we do not deal with them as if they were copies of ourselves. To recognize the relationships that occur between persons, their environments, and their actions is to act in compassion.

b. Participation involves the overlapping effect of our lives. It requires us to remember that we do not sin alone. Nor are we saved alone. The most innocent of acts—like the most violent ones—alter the nature of our environments so that they produce ethical dilemmas for us all.

c. Participation recognizes that the restraint of the immediate is the price we pay for the promise of the future. The long-term outcome of our activities are resident in immediate decisions.

d. Participation involves an awareness of dependency, the awesome recognition that who and what we are, as well as the fact *that* we are, is very much dependent on the willingness of others to allow it to happen. This emerges from the knowledge that we cannot (do not) supply our own necessities, our own food or shelter or clothing. As well, we realize that much of our security, our sense of home, and our acceptance in the community rests upon the openness and acceptance of others. We are not alone nor could we be. Others do not make our decisions nor are they responsible for me, but we are all dependent.

7. As a reasonable person I object to violence in any and every form. My objections are based first on the irrationality of it and, second, on the inhumanity of it. I agree with Mahatma Gandhi when he said "I object to violence because when it appears to do good, the good is only temporary; the evil is permanent." Personally I was trained—along with millions of other persons—to be violent. I learned during that period that when all else failed, violence has the tendency to get attention. We were taught that violence is a solution—albeit a bad one—to problems.

It is my feeling that much of the violence in this world comes as a result of not listening. We have not listened to minorities, we have not listened to the have-nots, we have not listened to the politically unhappy, we have not listened to our children, we have not listened to each other. And, when we can no longer stand to be ignored we step on someone's toe, hit them in the mouth, or blow them up. Our expectation of love, or search for human relationships, must somehow exclude this belief that the power to inflict pain or death or to control physically and mentally, carries with it the promise of victory.

233

8. Respect is lacking in the same manner that we have lacked restraint. Human relations are often irreparably upset by the lack of respect. It seems to emerge from a lack of attention for the situation in which persons are involved. It is more a case of not listening than of lack of care. But whatever the cause, the complaint is that *we are not heard,* that we make no difference, and that our opinions are of no value to anyone. Our respect for persons as persons and their points of view as points of view is the mortar which holds human life together. To neglect it is to do so at our peril.

Conclusion

It seems to be the case that the only ethics of any value to us is one that aids us in determining the difference between right and wrong. It would serve us in our decisions concerning good and bad. Such an ethic, however pragmatic or idealistic it might be, would be a principle (maybe even several) by which we could confront all value questions. It would serve to direct us as we deal with those everyday decisions about our behavior and allow us to determine in our selection what Brightman quotes as "the appearance of value and the reality of value."[3]

No matter how objective we become in our way of knowing, or how carefully we weigh the immediate irrationality of life against a metaphysical stability, sooner or later we will discover that we must make choices about the way we will act in given situations. There will be that point, or series of points, where the pressure will be on us to declare in works and in action what it is that we truly value. We will be called upon to express ourselves in actions that ultimately tell us what we ultimately love the most.[14]

If there is ever to be a time when a religious view is allowed to recapture our thoughts, or when free men and women will respond openly to the understandings of a morally meaningful life, then there will need to be some changes in the nature of religious thinking. The possibility of religion providing principles of ethical judgment depends a great deal on our ability to take an initiative. Bertrand Russell makes a strong statement in favor of this initiative.

The first and greatest change that is required is to establish a morality of initiative, not a morality of submission; a morality of hope rather than of fear; of things to be done rather than of things to be left undone....The religious life that we seek...will give praise to positive achievement rather than negative sinlessness, to the joy of life, the quick affection, the creative instinct, by which the world may grow young and beautiful and filled with vigor.[15]

End Notes

1. John Omar, *Grace and Personality* (New York: William Collins Sons and Company, Ltd., 1960), 122–123.
2. William Sloane Coffin, *The Courage to Be* (San Francisco: Harper and Row Publishers, 1982), 33.
3. Coffin, 33.
4. Dorothy Sayers, *The Mind of the Maker* (New York: The World Publishing Company, 1956), 178.
5. Jose Ortega y Gassett, *Man and Crisis* (New York: Norton Library, 1962), 16.
6. Bjarne Skard, *The Incarnation* (Minneapolis, Minnesota: Augsburg Publishing House, 1960), 25.
7. Crane Britton, *A History of Western Morals* (New York: Harcourt, Brace and Company, 1959), 5.
8. Coffin, 13.
9. F. Henry Edwards, *God Our Help* (Independence, Missouri: Herald Publishing House, 1943), 217.
10. John C. Bennett, *Christian Ethics and Social Policy* (Richmond: University of Virginia, 1945), 92.
11. Bennett, *Christian Ethics*, 66.
12. Norman Angell, *Why Freedom Matters* (Middlesex, England: Penguin Books, 1940), 105.

235

13. Brightman, *Moral Laws*, 29.
14. Michael Novak, *Ascent of the Mountain, Flight of the Dove* (New York: Harper and Row, 1978), 12.
15. Bertrand Russell, *Principles of Social Reconstruction* (London: Allen and Unwin, 1916), 203.

CHAPTER 13

BIBLIOGRAPHY

A book is the only place in which you can examine a fragile thought without breaking it, or explore an explosive idea without fear it will go off in your face. . . . It is one of the few havens remaining where a man's mind can get both provocation and privacy.

—Edward P. Morgan

I. General Works

Angell, Norman. *Why Freedom Matters.* Middlesex, England: Penguin Books, 1940.

Bach, Marcus. *The Power of Perception.* Garden City, New York: Doubleday and Company, Inc., 1966.

Banner, William A. *Ethics: An Introduction to Moral Philosophy.* New York: Charles Scribner's Sons, 1968.

Barth, Karl. *The Humanity of God.* Richmond: John Knox Press, 1960.

Bennett, John C. *Christian Ethics and Social Policy.* Richmond: University of Virginia, 1945.

Bentham, Jeremy. *Introduction to the Principles of Morals and Legislation* (1786). New York: Hafner Publishing Company, 1948.

Bonhoeffer, Dietrich. *The Cost of Discipleship.* Revised. New York: Macmillan, 1963.

Bradley, F. H. *Ethical Studies.* Indianapolis: Bobbs-Merrill, Company, 1951.

Brinton, Crane. *A History of Western Morals.* New York: Harcourt, Brace, and Company, 1959.

Brunner, Emil. *The Divine Imperative.* Philadelphia: Westminster Press, 1947.

Carritt, E. F. *The Theory of Morals.* London: Oxford University Press, 1930.

Christian, James. *Philosophy: An Introduction to the Art of Wondering.* Second Edition, New York: Holt, Rinehart, and Winston, 1977.

Devlin, Patrick. *The Enforcement of Morals.* Oxford: Oxford University Press, 1968.

Ducan-Jones, Austin. *Butler's Moral Philosophy.* Middlesex: Penguin Books, 1952.

Fletcher, Joseph. *Situation Ethics: The New Morality.* Philadelphia: The Westminster Press, 1960.

Flew, Anthony, (ed.). *A Dictionary of Philosophy.* New York: St. Martin's Press, 1979.

Frankena, William K. *Ethics.* New Jersey: Prentice-Hall, Inc., 1963.

Frankena, William K. and John Granrose. *Introductory Readings in Ethics.* New Jersey: Prentice-Hall, Inc., 1974.

Galbraith, Ronald and Thomas Jones. *Moral Reasoning.* Minnesota: Greenhaven Press, Inc., 1976.

Gasset, Jose Ortega Y. *Man and Crisis.* New York: Norton Library, 1962.

Gorovitz, Macklin, Jameton, O'Connor, and Sherwin. *Moral Problems in Medicine.* New Jersey: Prentice-Hall, Inc., 1983.

Harper, Ralph. *Nostalgia: An Existential Exploration of Longing and Fulfillment in the Modern World.* Cleveland: Western Reserve University Press, 1966.

Hollis, Martin. *Invitation to Philosophy.* Oxford: Basil Blackwell, Inc., 1985.

Huby, Pamela. *Greek Ethics.* New York: St. Martin's Press, 1967.

Hodgson, Peter and Robert King. *Christian Theology.* Philadelphia: Fortress Press, 1982.

Hugo, Victor. *Les Miserables.* 1862.

Kant, Immanuel. *Fundamental Principles of the Metaphysic of Morals.* Translated by Lewis W. Beck. Chicago: University of Chicago Press, 1949.

_____. *Critique of Pure Reason.* Translated by Lewis W. Beck. Chicago: University of Chicago Press, 1949.

Kurtz, Paul. *Moral Problems in Contemporary Society.* New Jersey: Prentice-Hall, Inc., 1969.

Lehmann, Paul L. *Ethics in a Christian Context.* New York: Harper and Row, Publishers, 1963.

Mackie, J. L. *Ethics: Inventing Right and Wrong.* Middlesex, England: Penguin Book, Ltd., 1985.

Mariet, Philip, (ed.). *Jean Paul Sartre: Existentialism and Humanism.* London: Negel and Methuen and Company, 1948.

Marty, Martin E. *The Place of Bonhoeffer: Problems and Possibilities in His Thought.* New York: The Association Press, 1962.

McClendon, James W. *Systematic Theology: Ethics.* Nashville: Abingdon Press, 1986.

Milgliore, Daniel L. *Called to Freedom.* Philadelphia: The Westminster Press, 1980.

Moore, G. E. *Principia Ethica.* Cambridge: Cambridge University Press, 1954.

Muller, Herbert J. *In Pursuit of Relevance.* Bloomington: Indiana University Press, 1971.

Niebuhr, Reinhold. *An Interpretation of Christian Ethics.* New York: Meridian Books, 1935.

Niebuhr, Reinhold. *The Children of Light and the*

Children of Darkness. New York: Meridian Books, 1960.

Nielsen, Kai. *Ethics Without God.* London: A Prometheus Book, 1973.

Novak, Michael. *Ascent of the Mountain, Flight of the Dove.* New York: Harper and Row, 1978.

Nowell-Smith, P. H. *Ethics.* Middlesex: Penguin Books, 1959.

Olson, Robert G. *A Short Introduction to Philosophy.* New York: Harcourt, Brace, and World, Inc., 1967.

Oman, John. *Grace and Personality.* New York: William Collins Sons and Company, Ltd., 1960.

Piaget, Jean. *Insights and Illusions of Philosophy.* New York: The World Publishing Company, 1972.

Purtill, Richard L. *Thinking About Ethics.* New Jersey: Prentice-Hall, Inc., 1976.

Reeck, Darrell. *Ethics for the Professions.* Minneapolis: Augsburg Publishing House, 1982.

Richman, H. P. *Preface to Philosophy.* London: Routledge and Kegan Paul, 1964.

Russell, Bertrand. *Principles of Social Reconstruction.* London: Allen and Unwin, 1916.

Sayers, Dorothy L. *The Mind of the Maker.* New York: Meridian Books, 1956.

Scriven, Michael. *Primary Philosophy.* New York: McGraw-Hill Book Company, 1966.

Shaw, Russell. *Choosing Well.* London: University of Notre Dame Press, 1982.

Skard, Bjarne. *The Incarnation.* Minneapolis: Augsburg Publishing House, 1960.

Smith, Joanmarie. *Morality Made Simple, But Not Easy.* Allen, Texas: Argus Communications, 1982.

Stein, Harry. *Ethics: And Other Liabilities.* New York: St. Martin's Press, 1982.

Torgerson, Jon and John Conovan. *Issues in Bio-Medical Ethics.* Iowa Humanities Grant Publication, 1977.

Weil, Simone. *Waiting for God.* New York: Harper and Row, Publishers, 1951.

Weinberg, Julius and Kieth Yandell. *Ethics.* New York: Holt, Rinehart, and Winston, Inc., 1971.

Woodhouse, Mark B. *A Preface to Philosophy.* Belmont, California: Wadsworth Publishing Company, 1984.

Woodyard, David O. *The Opaqueness of God.* Philadelphia: The Westminster Press, 1970.

II. RLDS: Herald House

Bolton, J. Andrew. *Restoring Persons in World Community.* 1986.

Clark, Marian and Daniel Fenn. *Human Sexuality.* Life Issues Series, 1982.

Committee on Basic Beliefs. *Exploring the Faith.* 1970.

Christian Education Office. *The Response of My People.* 1972.

Draper, Maurice. *Credo: "I Believe."* 1983.

Edwards, Nancy and Peter Judd. *Stewardship: The Response of My People.* 1976.

Edwards, F. Henry. *Life and Ministry of Jesus.* Revised. 1982.

Edwards, F. Henry. *God Our Help.* 1943.

Edwards, Paul. *Inquiring Faith: An Exploration in Religious Education.* 1967.

Elser, Otto. *The Ministry of Health and Healing.* 1986.

Howard, Barbara. *The Journey of Forgiveness.* 1986.

Judd, Peter and Daniel Fenn. *Pastoral Care: The*

Fruit of the Spirit. 1975.

Judd, Peter and Bruce Lindgren. *An Introduction to the Saints Church.* 1976.

Nowlin, Kathy. *Building Self-Esteem in the Family.* Life Issue Series. 1983.

Premoe, David and David Jewell. *Christian Vocation: The Call to Respond to the Gift of God's Love.* 1979.

Ruch, Velma. *The Signature of God: Religion in the World's Great Literature.* 1986.

Smith, Frederick M. *The Higher Powers of Man.* Reprinted, 1968.

Sparkes, Vernone. *The Theological Enterprise.* 1969.

Spencer, Geoffrey. *Strangers and Pilgrims: Images of the Church for Today.* 1984.

Troeh, Richard and Marjorie Troeh. *The Conferring Church.* 1986.

Yarrington, Roger. *Restoration Ethics Today.* 1963.

III. General Periodicals

Anonymous. "Equal, Not Really." *JAMA,* Vol. 254 (August 16, 1985): 953.

Brand, Paul and Philip Yancey. "Putting Pain to Work." *Leadership,* Fall Quarter, Vol. 4, No. 4 (1984): 121.

Carter, Nancy Corson. "The Prodigal Daughter: A Parable Re-Visioned." *Soundings,* Vol. 67, No. 1 (Spring 1985): 88.

Conference on Critical Thinking. Brochure, "Critical Thinking and Formation of Values." University of Chicago (November 1984).

Dodds, Harold. "The Importance of Being an Individual." *Wisdom* (July 1956): 53.

Edwards, Paul. "Leadership and Ethics of Prophecy." *Dialogue.* Vol. 19, No. 4 (1986): 77.

McMurrin, Sterling M. "Religion and the Denial of History." *Sunstone.* Vol. VII, No. 2 (March/April): 46.

Mesle, C. Robert. "The Problem of Genuine Evil: A Critique of John Hick's Theodicy." *The Journal of Religion.* Vol. 66, No. 4 (October 1986): 412.

O'Connor, June. "On Doing Religious Ethics." *Journal of Religious Ethics.* Vol. 7, No. 1 (Spring 1979): 81–95.

Outka, Gene. "Social Ethics and Equal Access to Health Care." *Journal of Religious Ethics.* Vol. 2, No. 1 (1974): 11–29.

Stackhouse, Max L. "Torture, Terrorism and Theology: The Need for a Universal Ethic." *The Christian Century.* (October 8, 1986): 861.

Thomas, Keith. "What Men Really Want: An Interview with Robert Bly." *New Age* (May 1982): 30.

IV. RLDS Periodicals

The *Saints Herald* (by date):

Burgess, A. A. "Revelation in Ethics and Religion." 68:147 (February 16, 1921).

"Newspaper Ethics." 68:627 (July 5, 1921).

"Newspaper Ethics. A Code." 68:914 (September 27, 1921).

Alkire, David. "A Problem in Ethics." 100:832 (August 31, 1953).

Wellington, Paul. "A New Profession: Counselor in Ethics." 110:146 (March 1963).

Stoft, Paul. "The Christian Ethic." 112:9 (January 1, 1965).

Townsend, Elsie. "Cheating." 112:692 (October 15, 1965).

Fitch, Richard E. "A Commonsense Sex Code." 112:336 (May 15, 1965).

"Justice Warren Calls for Institute on Laws, Ethics." 113:394 (June 1, 1966).

Shute, Evan. "Young People and Sex." 113:51 (January 15, 1966).

Mesle, Carl. "Our Men in Vietnam." 113:51 (February 1, 1966).

The First Presidency. "Statement on Objectives for the Church." 113:342 (May 15, 1966).

Connell, W. E. "Ethics and Morality." 113:589 (September 1, 1966).

Sparkes, Verne. "Sinful Man and the Civil Rights Dilemma." 113:690 (October 15, 1966).

Edwards, Lyman F. "Faith and Saintly Conduct." 114:258 (April 15, 1967).

Runkle, Jerry. "A Steward's Standard of Conduct." 120:24 (January 1973).

First Presidency. "Ethical Demands of Our Common Calling." 120:10 (March 1973).

Lindgren, Bruce. "Understanding Who We Are." 123:666 (November 1976).

Tyree, Alan D. "The Use of Wisdom." 124:494 (August 1977).

Booth, Paul W. "What in the World." 124:528 (September 1977).

Patton, Sharon. "Called to Community: A Theological Perspective" 126:66 (February 1979).

Swart, Margaret. "My Job Description as a Saint." 127:17 (January 1980).

Morgan, G. N. "Report to Chiefs of Staff: World Council." 127:480 (October 1980).

Best, Bruce. "With Enough Trust You Can Lose Your Arms." 128:60 (February 1981).

"A Scriptural Approach to Human Sexuality."
128:181 (April 1981).

"The Theological Meaning and Nature of Human
Sexuality." 128:224 (May 1981).

"Sex Roles and Variant Life-Styles." 128:286 (June
1981).

"Sexuality Education." 128:333 (July 1981).

The First Presidency. "Conference Organization,
Peace and Nuclear Arms." 129:263 (June 1982).

"Ministerial Perspective on Abortion." 131:496
(November 1984).

Higdon, Barbara. "A Community of Conviction."
134:95 (March 1987).

Autumn Leaves

Smith, Fred M. "The Great Ethical Law" 21:535
(December 1908).

Smith, Elbert A. "Ethics for Young People." 21:563
(December 1908).

Stride

Shute, Evan. "Advancing Through the Minefields."
10:224 (June 1966).

University Bulletin

Atlantic States College Student and Young Adult
Conference. "The Restoration in a Tangled
World." 19:4:58 (Spring 1967).

Croft, Joyce. "The Obligated Education" 6:3:14
(May 1954).

McDowell, Dr. F. M. "Let's Define Righteousness."
7:1:3 (December 1954).

Mathews, Joseph W. "The Revolutionary Man."
20:2–3:1 (Winter 1964).

Morris, Harley A. "Faith Rationality in Kingdom Building." 10:4; 5 (Spring 1958).

V. Incidental and Unpublished Works

Edwards, Paul. "Ethics and Dissent in Mormonism." Sunstone Theological Symposium, Salt Lake City (August 1986).

Edwards, Paul. "Lying and Hiding in America: Sometimes Bad is Bad." Park College Convocation Series (February 1987).

Tyree, Alan. "Divine Calling in Human History." 1984 W. Wallace Smith Lecture at Park College (March 1, 1984).

"Universal Declaration of Human Rights." United Nations General Assembly Resolution 217-III-A (December 10, 1948).